THE U.F.O. PHENOMENON

By the same author

JOURNEY TO INFINITY

TIME-SLIP

THE
U.F.O.
PHENOMENON

JOHANNES VON BUTTLAR

Translated by Nicholas Fry

SIDGWICK & JACKSON

LONDON

ISBN 0 283 98538 0
Printed in Great Britain by
A. Wheaton & Co., Ltd., Exeter

for Sidgwick and Jackson Limited
1 Tavistock Chambers, Bloomsbury Way
London WC1A 2SG

Photosetting by Rainbow Graphics, Liverpool

Acknowledgements

Thanks are due to all those who have contributed directly or indirectly to the writing of this book: this includes the American organizations, the Center for U.F.O. Studies; National Investigations Committee on Aerial Phenomena (N.I.C.A.P.); Aerial Phenomenon Research Organization (A.P.R.O.) and Mutual U.F.O. Network (M.U.F.O.N.); the U.S. Air Force; *Flying Saucer Review*, London; Deutsche U.F.O. und I.F.O. Studien Gesellschaft – German U.F.O. and Identified Flying Objects Study Society (D.U.I.S.T.), the Federal Republic of Germany and (willingly or unwillingly) the C.I.A. and the K.G.B.

Special thanks are due to Professor Allen J. Hynek and Major Donald E. Keyhoe (Ret.) for their fearless pioneer work in a field which is unfortunately still in disrepute.

Nor must I forget Charles Bowen; Dr Walter K. Bühler; Gordon Creighton; W. Raymond Drake; Professor David Michael Jacobs; John A. Keel; Coral and Jim Lorenzen; Aimé Michel; Professor David Saunders; Dr Jacques Vallee and Karl L. Veit, among many others.

I am particularly grateful to my friends, Ellida Baroness von Stetten, Richard Giese, our dear 'Nippi', and most of all my

5

friend of long standing, Timothy Good, and to my wife Elis' for providing invaluable help and advice.

And thanks not least to all those 'daring flying saucers', without which this book, needless to say, could not have existed.

Contents

Foreword

It was only after long and intense deliberation that I decided to write this report on the background to the world-wide phenomenon of unidentified flying objects.

It is a subject which arouses highly conflicting emotions and any discussion of it can only provide fuel for these conflicts. There can be no other theme which is so thoroughly beset by prejudice and supposition, by doubts and overstatements, falsifications and even intrigue.

It is a subject on which there can be no compromise, only the two extremes of for and against.

There are innumerable accounts from all over the world of confrontations with unidentified flying objects. According to one survey, in America alone some 15 million people – including President Jimmy Carter – claim to have seen U.F.O.s. Such a phenomenon deserves our attention, however we care to categorize it. And as it is a writer's task to seek out the truth, this is the object which I have set myself here.

. The search for truth in such a field as this is inevitably full of dangers; it is a test of courage for both author and reader. For the author it demands a willingness to reveal the truth once he has discovered it, and for the reader, a willingness to set aside his preconceived ideas. JOHANNES VON BUTTLAR

9

1
Tracks

On the road to Coral Gables, a small provincial town in Florida, a patrol car of the Dade county police drove for the second time past the carelessly parked station wagon.

'Something's wrong here. Pull over!' said the officer in the passenger seat, suspiciously, to his colleague at the wheel.

When the two patrolmen opened the door of the station wagon, at 6.30 on the evening of 20 April 1959, they found the figure of a man slumped over the wheel. He was obviously dead, and a tube leading from the exhaust pipe to the interior of the car told its own story.

The subsequent police inquiry pronounced a verdict of suicide through acute carbon monoxide poisoning.

The identity of the corpse, too, was quickly revealed, when one of the patrolmen found some personal papers in the dead man's pocket.

'Dr Morris K. Jessup,' he read out to his colleague, 'born on 2 March 1900 in Indiana.'

'Jessup? Did you say Jessup?' The other man sounded puzzled. 'Not Professor Jessup. The one involved in the U.F.O. affair? Why ever should he want to kill himself?'

This question was to be asked more than once in the years to come, and to induce the wildest suppositions. For if Jessup's death was puzzling enough in itself, the circumstances which preceded it were even stranger.

What had driven Dr Jessup, a highly qualified astrophysicist, to take his own life?

Not only had he taught astronomy and mathematics as a professor at Michigan and Drake Universities, he had also been responsible for the construction and operation of the largest refracting telescope in the southern hemisphere, in South Africa. It was to Jessup that the world owed the discovery of a whole series of binary stars.

And this was not all; even the U.S. Department of Agriculture made use of Jessup's talents, commissioning him to investigate potential sources of raw rubber in the Amazonas region in South America.

But Jessup's life was changed radically by the sight of a pulsating disc - a light which appeared suddenly in the sky. Whether this event dates from his stay in South Africa or in South America can no longer be established, but as he once admitted to a friend, it changed the course of his life. And there are many people who believe that it also led to his mysterious death.

As reports of U.F.O. sightings multiplied all over the world, Jessup became increasingly preoccupied by this bewildering phenomenon. He began to study the U.F.O. reports systematically, classifying them, analysing them and evaluating them with scientific exactitude. It soon became apparent to him that a relatively high percentage of U.F.O. sightings could not be explained away by human error or imagination or deliberate deception. In his opinion, U.F.O.s were nothing more or less than Unidentified Flying Objects.

It was in the summer of 1947 that humanity was first presented with the amazing concept of 'flying saucers', which ushered in a new age and was to provide fuel for speculation for decades to come.

Strangely, it was a relatively unspectacular U.F.O. sighting which inaugurated this new era. It is not quite clear why this particular event should have caused the furore it did. Perhaps it was merely the use of the term 'flying saucer' for the first time. But for journalists all over the world it was a godsend, a term which exactly described the bewildering phenomenon. U.F.O.s were flying saucers! And as saucers do not normally fly, reporters could add a pleasant touch of irony to their accounts. Not surprisingly, 'flying saucer' soon became the popular term for U.F.O. sightings all over the world.

'It would have been disloyal to my country not to report this sighting,' said Kenneth Arnold to reporters on 24 June 1947. Arnold, the president of a firm which manufactured fire extinguishers in Boise, Idaho, piloted his own aeroplane, and on the afternoon of 14 June, at 2 o'clock, he had taken off from Chehalis airfield, Washington, bound for Yakima, Washington.

According to a report by the U.S. Air Force Board of Inquiry, Arnold's planned flight had been interrupted for an hour while he took part in the search for a Navy transport plane which had apparently crashed from nearly 10,000 feet near or south-west of Mount Rainier – roughly at the height of the plateau which projects from the mountain. After about an hour's fruitless search, Arnold resumed his original route towards Yakima.

'That day the weather was so good that flying was sheer pleasure,' Arnold reported.

He trimmed his machine and sat back comfortably to watch the sky and the landscape gliding past beneath him. On his left and behind him, he noticed a DC-4 travelling at about 15,000 feet.

Arnold had hardly been on his original course for more than two or three minutes when a blinding beam of light was reflected by his aircraft. At first he could not make out the source of this reflection. Then he was surprised to see a row of strange flying objects on his left, to the north of Mount Rainier, flying south at about 10,000 feet. Judging by the speed with which they approached Mount Rainier, Arnold thought that they must be jets.

Two or three of the flying objects banked or altered their course every few seconds so that they were struck by the sunlight. As they were fairly far away from Arnold, he could not make out either their shapes or their formation. But as they approached Mount Rainier, their shapes became gradually clearer. At the official inquiry, Arnold stated that he had been unable to make out any tail on the machines, but he had assumed that they were some kind of jet aircraft. They were flying at roughly the same height as himself, on a level with the horizon, and moving up and down by about a thousand feet.

The objects were flying strung out in a diagonal line, almost as if they were joined together. They held a definite course, but swerved round the summit of the mountain. Arnold estimated their distance as being about sixteen miles from his aircraft and their size as about two-thirds that of a DC-4. As they flew over a snow-covered chain of peaks, he observed that the first U.F.O. passed over the southern peak of the chain, while the last reached the northernmost peak.

Later measurements of the ridge showed that the line of U.F.O.s must have been about five miles long.

Some fifty miles south of Mount Rainier is Mount Adams. Arnold timed the U.F.O.s between these two points and counted one minute forty-two seconds – representing a speed of over 1,750 m.p.h.

They sailed through the crystal-clear air 'like *saucers* skimming over water', Arnold told reporters on the evening of 14 June.

Only a few hours after his arrival in Yakima, he was already being bombarded with questions by the press. Journalist's intuition told them that here was a mystery which would make headlines for some time to come.

Who had Arnold encountered? What were these 'saucers'?

Had Arnold stumbled on some new kind of aircraft, secretly developed by the U.S. Air Force? Or were they really alien flying machines from the depths of nowhere? In either case it was clearly something to be taken seriously. One 'thing was certain – Arnold was no sensation-monger, but a respectable businessman and an experienced pilot. Altogether it made ideal copy for the newspapers.

Judging by the headlines of the Arnold sighting, U.F.O.s were a new and hitherto unknown phenomenon. But this was not quite true. Unidentified flying objects have been reported over and over again throughout history.

During the Second World War, for example, pilots on both sides were repeatedly accompanied on their missions by strange disc-shaped flying objects. The Allied bomber pilots christened the objects 'foo fighters'. They were said to have extraordinary speed and manoeuverability, flipping to and fro across the bombers' flight-paths and flying ahead or astern of them on the same course. Even the crews on warships witnessed the antics of these amazing craft. At first the Allies thought they were a phenomenon produced by electrical discharges in the atmosphere. Then the rumour spread that the Germans or Japanese had introduced a new secret weapon designed to upset the ignition systems of the bombers. But as the foo fighters did not indulge in any hostile tactics, many flight crews became convinced that the enemy had gone over to psychological warfare and was sending up these devices to unnerve the English and American pilots.

Ironically, it was not until the end of the war that the American public learned that Japanese and German pilots had encountered the same phenomenon. They too had been convinced that they were dealing with a secret enemy weapon.

In any case the foo fighters were taken seriously enough for the American 8th Army to order a thorough investigation of the phenomenon. This investigation pronounced them to be the result of mass hallucination, since no known military power possessed the technological resources necessary for building such craft. And with that the matter was dropped, especially since the foo fighters behaved in a peaceful manner. Their origin has not been explained to this day.

After the end of the Second World War, a former B-17 pilot, Charles Odom, described his encounters with foo fighters in the autumn and winter of 1944–5 over Germany. 'They looked like crystal balls, clear and about the size of basketballs,' he said. They were observed particularly often over Munich, Vienna and other important bombing targets. They would approach to within 300 feet of a bomber formation, then 'would seem to become magnetized to our formation and fly alongside. They never came closer than 300 feet. After a while they would peel off like a plane and leave.'

As Jessup became more and more involved in his private investigation, he began to receive increasing numbers of reports of sightings which friends, colleagues and pilots remembered and communicated to him in confidence.

Until 1947, observations of this kind had aroused remarkably little excitement among the general public. But with the Arnold sighting the floodgates seemed to open. Suddenly, all over the world, men were talking about what they had seen or thought they had seen. Many of them, inevitably, were talking about things which they had not seen at all.

What two United Airlines pilots experienced on 4 July 1947, however, was obviously reality. They were taking off in their airliner from Boise, Idaho, on their way to Seattle, Washington.

Flight Captain Emil J. Smith was sitting at the controls with co-pilot Ralph Stevens next to him. Shortly before take-off the two men had been asked by reporters what they thought of flying saucers and Smith had replied that he would believe in them only when he saw one with his own eyes.

Eight minutes later the United Airlines machine was over Emmett, Idaho. It had reached its cruising altitude of about 8,000 feet when Smith sighted what he imagined to be an aircraft in front of him. He switched on the landing lights and their powerful beams lit up the way ahead.

Smith later told reporters that he had at first assumed that it was merely a formation of light aircraft which he had seen in front of him, but then he had realized that they were no ordinary aircraft, but flat, round flying objects. Wishing to have some verification, Smith and Stevens called the stewardess into the cockpit. Without telling her the reason, they asked her to look at the sky outside. She noticed the U.F.O.s immediately. It was 9.15 p.m. and the evening sky was still light, so that the objects flying ahead of the United Airlines machine stood out as uncannily large, grey silhouettes – 'smooth underneath and rough on top', as Smith described them.

Flight Captain Smith called up the control tower at Ontario, Oregon, and after giving his position, asked whether there was anything unusual in the sky on his course. When the flight controller was unable to make out anything near the position given, Smith concluded that the U.F.O.s must be much further off and larger than he had estimated.

The U.F.O.s seemed to melt together before disappearing from view in a north-westerly direction.

But that was not all. No sooner had the first group disappeared than a second group appeared ahead of them on the port side. The objects were flying in a row, three of them close together with a fourth following some distance behind. Just like the first, this second formation suddenly shot away at high speed.

After receiving 156 official reports, the U.S. Air Force came to the conclusion that the methods used by the A.M.C. (Air Material Command) in investigating the U.F.O. problem were no longer adequate for the task.

On 23 September 1947, Lieutenant General Nathan F. Twining, Commander in Chief of the A.M.C., sent a top secret report to the general commanding the U.S. Army Air Force, in which he classified the U.F.O. phenomenon as real and emphasized that the sightings could not be dismissed as fantasy or fairy-tales. The objects, he stated, were apparently disc-shaped, were of the size of aircraft, and must be steered manually or automatically, or by remote control.

The text of Twining's secret report runs as follows:

1. As requested by AC/AS-2, there is presented below the considered opinion of this Command concerning the so-called 'Flying Discs'. . . . This opinion was arrived at in a conference between personnel of the Air Institute of Technology, Intelligence, T-2, Office, Chief of Engineering Division, and the Aircraft, Power Plant and Propeller Laboratories of Engineering Division T-3.

2. It is the opinion that:

a. The phenomenon reported is something real and not visionary or fictitious.

b. There are objects probably approximating the shape of a disc of such appreciable size as to appear to be as large as man-made aircraft.

c. There is a possibility that some of the incidents may be caused by natural phenomena, such as meteors.

d. The reported operating characteristics such as extreme rates of climb, manoeuverability (particularly in roll), and action which must be considered evasive when sighted or contacted by friendly aircraft and radar, lend belief to the possibility that some of the objects are controlled either manually, automatically or remotely.

e. The apparently common description of the objects is as follows:

(1) Metallic or light reflecting surface.

(2) Absence of trail, except in a few instances when the object apparently was operating under high-performance conditions.

(3) Circular or elliptical in shape, flat on bottom and domed on top.

(4) Several reports of well kept formation flights varying from three to nine objects.

(5) Normally no associated sound, except in three instances a substantial rumbling roar was heard.

(6) Level flight speeds normally above 300 knots are estimated.

3. It is recommended that: a. Headquarters, Army Air Force issue a directive assigning a priority, security classification and code name for a detailed study of this matter . . .

4. Awaiting a specific directive A.M.C. will continue the investigation within its current resources . . .

> N.F. Twining,
> Lieutenant General, U.S.A.
> Commanding.

It was on the basis of this report that the secret U.F.O. Project Sign was brought into being by the U.S. Air Force.

2
Fatal Encounter

In answer to the top-secret report submitted by Twining, Major General C.L. Craigie ordered the founding of an Air Force project to investigate the phenomenon of unidentified flying objects.

Project Sign was assigned to the Wright-Patterson Air Force base, classified as a grade 2A secret and placed under the command of the Technical Intelligence Division of the A.M.C.

Project Sign, or Project Saucer, as it was also called by the initiated, began its work on 22 January 1948. This involved, first of all, the collection of all information about U.F.O. sightings and phenomena in the atmosphere in so far as these could affect the national security of the United States. They then had to be compared, evaluated, and finally submitted to certain governmental authorities. The main task of the secret project was to establish whether U.F.O.s represented a threat to national security.

Two weeks before the project was set in motion, a particularly extraordinary U.F.O. sighting brought the American public to the brink of mass hysteria. The repercussions of the incident were to keep Project Sign busy for almost a year.

On 7 January 1948, eyewitnesses saw a silvery, disc-shaped object over Louisville, Kentucky, from which shone a reddish light. It had a diameter of some 250 to 300 feet and was flying in a southerly direction. The state police immediately alerted the Godman Air Force Base at Fort Knox and fifteen minutes later the crew in the control tower there sighted the U.F.O. When they were sure that it was neither an aircraft nor a weather balloon, they alerted the duty officer, the intelligence officer, and finally the base commander, Colonel Guy F. Hix. The latter contacted Captain Thomas Mantell by radio and ordered him to go up with his flight of F-51s to investigate.

The twenty-five-year-old flight captain was a highly qualified pilot and had already been decorated with the Distinguished Flying Cross in the Second World War. In fact, Mantell had been one of the first pilots to fly on the bombing raids on German positions at Cherbourg, which had inaugurated the Anglo-American invasion of Europe.

When Mantell took off in pursuit of the U.F.O. on that early afternoon of 7 January, he was accompanied by Lieutenants Hendricks, Clements and Hammond. Watchers on the ground followed the course of the fighters on their radar screens until at around 3 o'clock Mantell came in on the radio: 'Can't see anything yet, turning towards Ohio River Falls. Out.'

15.02 Mantell: 'Visibility 100 per cent. Not a thing in sight. Flying height 28,000 feet. Still climbing. Out.'

15.09: 'Reached 28,000 feet. Nothing in sight.'

15.11: 'Mantell here. Now I've got it! It's a disc, enormously large. Hard to say, could be 80 yards in diameter. Upper surface has a ring and a dome. Turning fantastically fast, apparently round a central vertical axis. My altimeter reads 31,500 feet. Out.'

There was feverish activity in the control tower. The radar observers stared as if hypnotized at their screens. There it was – an enormous disc!

15.12 The right wing pilot came in: 'I can see the disc. Am photographing it. Mantell's behind. About 200 feet above me. Left wing pilot falling in. Attempting to pursue.'

15.14 Mantell: 'Another thousand yards and I've got it. Flying twice as fast. I'm overtaking the thing. It's got a metallic gleam. It's shrouded in yellowish light – now the colour's changing, becoming reddish – orange-coloured.

15.15: Just 400 yards to go. Disc speeding up. Trying to escape. Climbing at about forty-five degrees. Out.'

15.16 Message from the right wing pilot: 'Mantell's almost got it, only a couple of yards more. Disc is putting on a spurt. Can't keep up. Out.'

Hammond and Clements now gave up and asked permission to land, as Mantell had disappeared from view. Hendricks had already returned to the base.

15.18 Mantell: 'The thing's gigantic. It's flying unbelievably fast. I can see windows. Now . . .'

That was the last which was heard of Mantell. At about 4 o'clock in the afternoon a search party which had been sent out as soon as he broke radio contact found the wreckage of his plane scattered over an area nearly a mile across. Mantell's watch had stopped at 15.18.

Naturally the press made sensational copy out of the incident. A strange light appearing in the night sky is one thing. But the death of an experienced pilot in circumstances associated with a 'flying saucer' is quite another, especially when it happens in broad daylight.

The public became uneasy. Even some of the people who had hitherto dismissed the U.F.O. phenomenon with a sarcastic smile began to feel pangs of anxiety. What had previously been just a mysterious, unknown presence in the sky was now showing signs of hostility. Had Mantell gone in pursuit of an extra-terrestrial spaceship manned by hostile beings? Or was it a new and secret weapon invented by the Russians? The whole subject was fraught with mystery.

The Air Force and the investigation team of Project Sign were equally bewildered. At least that seems the only possible excuse for the ludicrous explanation which they put out in an attempt to quieten the press and reduce public anxiety. Their statement was simple and dramatic: Mantell had gone in pursuit of the planet Venus and had perished in the attempt to catch up with a planet millions of miles away in space. When astronomers and scientists rejected this theory, observing that the sky had been cloudy at the time and that Venus had been practically invisible on the date in question, especially by daylight, another equally limp explanation was offered. This time Mantell was said to have gone in pursuit of a skyhook – a reconnaissance balloon. In a subsequent investigation by the A.T.I.C. (Air Technical Intelligence Center), however, it was proved that no skyhooks could have been in the area at the time. It was one of the A.T.I.C.s tasks to record all launchings of reconnaisance balloons. Moreover on that extraordinary day an engineer named Scott had been at Godman Field, and according to him Mantell's final statement had been: 'Good God, it's enormous. It's got windows.'

Scott maintains that he personally listened to the tape-recording of Mantell's last radio message, but in the subsequent official report this last observation was missing.

Not surprisingly, Professor Jessup found the Mantell case particularly interesting. He ruled out from the beginning the possibility that some new secret type of aircraft was involved, for he was in no doubt that no power on earth was capable of building a craft with the characteristics observed of the U.F.O.s. No one had the technology to produce machines with their manoeuverability, their astonishing acceleration, their capacity to make ninety-degree turns. It was quite simply inconceivable. The available evidence could lead to only one conclusion – that U.F.O.s are of extraterrestrial origin and operate with the help of technologies which are light-years ahead of anything available on earth. Without a doubt Mantell had gone in pursuit of such an extraterrestrial machine. Perhaps he had gone too near to it and got caught in some force field related to its propulsion system which had blown his aircraft to pieces.

Interestingly enough, the investigators working on Project Sign had come to similar conclusions – as was shown by their subsequent secret reports.

As an astronomer, Jessup knew that the possibility of extra-terrestrial life is overwhelmingly great. It would be almost madness to consider mankind as the only intelligent life form in the Universe. Our solar system is by no means unique, in fact it is just one of innumerable similar planetary systems.

Life – in whatever form it appears – is dependent on complex, rapidly changing chemical links. Temperature plays a vital part in these chemical transformations, since extremes of either heat or cold will prevent them from taking place. Thus the evolution of higher life forms depends on three basic conditions:

1. A star which provides the required temperature, the ecosphere, for a sufficient length of time.
2. A planet which is at least as old as the Earth – i.e. some 5,000 million years – long enough for the origin and evolution of life to have taken place.
3. A suitable environment – the biosphere – in which life can be maintained.

It has been estimated that in our own galaxy, the Milky Way, there are thousands of millions of stars on which life must exist. And it can be safely assumed that life and intelligence of one kind or another exist in the Universe wherever there has been sufficient time and a suitable environment for its development. In fact the Milky Way must contain life at all stages of development – life which is still at the beginnings of creation relative to our own, or which conversely is millions of years ahead of us. On the Cosmic scale there is little difference between 5,000 or 50,000 years of development.

It would surely be one of the major aims of highly developed intelligences to investigate not only their own, immediate world, but also unknown worlds – to explore the Universe and make contact with alien intelligence.

It was thoughts of this kind for which Jessup considered that he found some confirmation in the U.F.O. sightings.

On 6 April 1948 scientists observed an oval-shaped U.F.O. over the White Sands missile range in New Mexico. After taking theodolite measurements they calculated its speed at about 17,000 m.p.h. When the U.F.O. suddenly rose steeply, its rate of climb was measured – again by theodolites – at twenty-five miles in ten seconds.

On 2 July 1948 about ten people saw eight unidentified flying objects, which passed over the township of Disma and landed on a rise in the neighbourhood of St Maries, Idaho.

On the evening of the same day radio announcer Dannie Kelley saw a similar formation of U.F.O.s flying rapidly over his home town of Augusta, Maine. The objects seemed to be grey and were flying faster than any aircraft Kelley had ever seen. It was later discovered that U.F.O.s had appeared at the same time in thirty-three different American states. In Knoxville, Professor C.E. Brehm of the University of Tennessee observed a long, metallic-looking cylinder moving rapidly across the sky.

On 24 July 1948 at 2.45 in the morning, a DC-3 of Eastern Air Lines was flying between Mobile and Montgomery, Alabama, when Flight Captain C. Chiles and his co-pilot, J. Whitted, simultaneously noticed a dull red light some 300 yards ahead of them, and remarked that it must be one of the new military jets they had heard about.

The object seemed to be approaching the DC-3 in a shallow dive, but suddenly banked left and passed to the right of the aircraft, at the same height and parallel to its course.

At this point the pilots of the DC-3 estimated the distance of the object at about 900 yards. After it had passed the airliner, it climbed at a steep angle and disappeared into a cloud. Violent shock waves tossed the heavy DC-3 from side to side. Later, Chiles and Whitted described the object as wingless, some 115 feet long, cigar-shaped and at least twice the diameter of a B-29. There seemed to be no lifting surfaces or rudder, but something resembling a radar antenna was protruding at the front. Chiles also had the impression of seeing a cabin with windows. The object seemed to be extraordinarily brightly lit inside. As it slid past, the two pilots noticed that the body of the object gleamed with a dark blue phosphorescence along its entire length. An orange-coloured trail stretched behind it.

It transpired that there was another pilot flying in the area at the time, and he reported having seen a brightly shining object in the sky. Eyewitnesses on the ground, too, had seen a similar object in the sky at the time of the DC-3's encounter with the U.F.O.

A remarkably similar occurrence had taken place two years earlier, on 1 August 1946. On that day, Captain Jack E. Puckett, a former Second World War bomber pilot and at the time chief air traffic control officer to the Tactical Air Command, was flying a C-47 transport with a co-pilot and flight engineer from his base at Langley Field, Virginia, to McDill. Thirty miles from Tampa, Florida, the three men saw a large U.F.O. speeding towards them on a collision course.

'At about a thousand yards it veered to cross our path. We observed it to be a long, cylindrical shape approximately twice the size of a B-29 bomber.' The machine left a trail of fire behind it and disappeared at an estimated speed of 1,500 to 2,000 m.p.h.

But, for the Air Force experts, the most amazing thing about this encounter was that the crew of the C-47 claimed to have seen a row of 'portholes' on the side of the object. If the U.F.O. had windows, that must mean it had a crew, consisting of beings who had eyes.

Almost three years later, on 1 November 1948, radar observers at the Goose Bay air base in Labrador saw a strange flying object which passed through their airspace at about 600 m.p.h.

Two days after this, radar operators of the Japanese Air Force followed two flying objects for over an hour as they apparently engaged in airborne combat. On the radar screens they looked like aircraft, but there were no conventional machines in the area at the time.

Three weeks later German airspace controllers were presented with another mystery. In the night of 23 November, an F-80 jet fighter encountered a rotating object with bright red lights, 30,000 feet above Fürstenfeldbruck in Bavaria. Radar observers on the ground noticed the U.F.O. at the same time. When the fighter approached it, the glowing red object rose rapidly out of sight, but before it disappeared from the radar screens its height was calculated to be 43,000 feet.

'All these incidents created confusion,' to quote the later comment of Professor Allen J. Hynek of the Department of Astronomy at Northwestern University, Evanston, Illinois. Besides being an astrophysicist, Hynek was also employed by the U.S. Air Force as an adviser on U.F.O.s.

Such confusion was understandable. Too many of the U.F.O. sightings, from all over the world, were being reported by unquestionably responsible people – mountain rescue pilots, police officials, airline pilots and military air traffic controllers.

The U.S. Air Force, entrusted with the air defence of the nation, felt itself under direct attack.

Inevitably, there were people who were only too ready to explain the phenomenon in terms of a threat to national security, some secret weapon invented by a foreign power. This was something the military mind could grasp immediately. However alarming it might be, at least it could possibly be combated.

But the observed characteristics of the U.F.O.s lay nowhere within the bounds of possible military invention – and only a small percentage of the sightings could be ascribed with any certainty to astronomical objects or events.

As a result, opinions in Project Sign were very soon divided. Were they dealing with extraterrestrial or merely terrestrial, but foreign, technology? Were the objects really extraterrestrial spaceships or merely the result of a mass psychosis – a kind of postwar neurosis?

The conventional explanations soon ran out. Finally, there were only two possibilities. Either the problem had to be psychological – a solution which was embraced only too willingly in the absence of more convincing explanations. Or the phenomenon was the visible evidence of something which no one wanted to admit.

As soon as the human mind is confronted with facts which do not fit into its normal vision of the world, it struggles to overcome the discrepancy. And it usually enlists the help of emotion rather than intellect, since intellect would have to admit a gap in its knowledge.

In 1948 Project Sign found itself in the lamentable situation of being unable to provide any satisfactory explanation for U.F.O.s and so it turned to its scientific advisers in the Air Force and the scientific establishment. And there it was promptly decided that what ought not to exist does not exist.

The U.S. Air Force played a key role, and the rest of the world, i.e. other governments, took their cue from what it had to say. Hynek comments:

> When I asked what was being done in those countries about the U.F.O. problem, on many occasions I was told that since the United States, with all its funds and facilities, was handling the problem, what more could other countries do with their limited facilities? They would await the outcome of the U.S. investigation.

For months on end the staff of Project Sign analysed the available evidence: interrogations of pilots, radar pictures, observations by scientists and specially qualified witnesses.

The picture which emerged was as follows. Most U.F.O.s are disc-shaped, usually with a dome on top, and have a diameter ten times their thickness in the centre. They frequently fly in formation and are observed both by eyewitnesses and radar. There are also elliptical or cigar-shaped objects, a few of them 'double-deckers', with two rows of windows, one above the other. Both types have extraordinary powers of acceleration, are fantastically fast and can make 180 degree turns in flight. They obviously use revolutionary propulsion methods which are far superior to any known on earth.

The scientists and intelligence officers on the project came to the unanimous, and highly secret, conclusion that U.F.O.s are extraterrestrial spaceships which are observing the earth for reasons unknown to us. They produced a detailed report which was submitted to General Hoyt S. Vandenberg, the Air Force Chief of Staff at the time. The conclusion to this top secret document, No. F-TR-2274-IA runs as follows:

3. Spaceships: The following considerations pertain:

   (a)   If there is an extraterrestrial civilization which can make such objects as are reported then it is most probable that its development is far in advance of ours. This argument can be supported on probability arguments alone without recourse to astronomical hypotheses.

(b) Such a civilization might observe that on earth we now have atomic bombs and are fast developing rockets. In view of the past history of mankind, they should be alarmed. We should, therefore, expect at this time above all to behold such visitations.

Since the acts of mankind most easily observed from a distance are A-bomb explosions, we should expect some relation to obtain between the time of A-bomb explosions, the time at which spaceships are seen, and the time required for such ships to arrive from and return to home base.

The report also suggested to General Vandenberg that the U.S. Air Force should train personnel specially for the purpose of solving the U.F.O. problem. At the same time the use of new techniques in radar and photography was recommended, so that more exact data on the sightings could be obtained.

The report's 1A security classification meant that not many people saw it, but for those who did the cat was out of the bag. Project Sign was in little doubt that U.F.O.s were extra-terrestrial spaceships observing the earth and that they were engaged in a long-term investigation of the planet.

The question which now arose was whether the public should be informed. The members of the Project were wholeheartedly in favour, and also tried to convince the General that it would be better to inform the nation immediately than to wait until some misfortune brought matters into the open. But General Hoyt S. Vandenberg had different ideas. He read the report and said two words: 'Burn it!'

In explanation of his decision, he stated that the public anxiety which would follow publication of the report was not to be contemplated. Moreover there was no solid physical proof of its assertions. Quite apart from this, how could the public be made to understand that the U.F.O.s were not hostile when no one could be sure that this was so? The result could only be panic.

And so the report went up in flames – except for one copy which someone had 'forgotten'.

3

Evasive Tactics

Shortly after the Project Sign report, another expert opinion was produced by Dr James E. Lipp, of the missile department of the Rand Corporation in Santa Monica, California. It was addressed to Brigadier General Putt, then the Air Force's Director of Research and Development, and dealt with the subject of U.F.O.s as extraterrestrial spaceships.

In his report of 13 December 1948, Lipp stated that these flying objects could not have originated from a planet in our solar system, since Earth was the only one which supported intelligent life. If they were in fact real, they would therefore have to come from some other planetary system. But even if some civilization in another planetary system had developed space travel, the distances between such a system and our own was too great for such a journey to be feasible. Lipp still did not rule out the possibility of visits by extraterrestrial beings, even though they seemed to him unlikely.

Lipp also argued that if extraterrestrial beings did come, they would surely make contact with men.

His statement that the flying objects which had been observed did not correspond to his concept of a spaceship is puzzling, since one statement in his report seems to suggest some of the observed characteristics of U.F.O.s:

Two possibilities are thus presented. First, a number of spaceships could have come as a group. This would only be done if full-dress contact were to be established. Second, numerous small craft might descend from a mother ship which coasts around the earth in a satellite orbit. But this could mean that the smaller craft would have to be rockets of satellite performance, and to contain them the mother ship would have to be truly enormous.

After the Project Sign report, the U.S. Air Force drastically altered its attitude towards U.F.O.s. And with this change in policy, the name of the project was significantly changed to 'Grudge'.

Suddenly U.F.O.s had become a lot of nonsense. The analysts of Project Grudge had to start from the premise that all U.F.O. sightings were the result of deliberate deception, hallucination or misidentification. In the words of Allen Hynek, writing in his book *The U.F.O. Experience*, 'The climate toward any serious investigation of flying saucers had become very chilly.' Hynek goes on to quote Captain Edward Ruppelt, the intelligence officer dealing with U.F.O. sightings by the Air Force, as saying:

This drastic change in official attitude is as difficult to explain as it was difficult for many people who knew what was going on inside Project Sign to believe ... Everything was being evaluated on the premise that U.F.O.s couldn't exist ... Good U.F.O. reports continued to come in at the rate of about ten per month, but they weren't being verified or investigated. Most of them were being discarded.

In the same book, Hynek comments:

The change to Project Grudge signaled the adoption of the strict brush-off attitude to the U.F.O. problem. Now the public relations statements on specific U.F.O. cases bore little resemblance to the facts of the case. If a case contained some of the elements possibly attributable to aircraft, a balloon, etc., it automatically became that object in the press release.

If this new U.F.O. policy was incomprehensible to many of the initiated, there were good reasons for it. But those reasons were known only to a few people in the upper echelons of the government and the Secret Service, and uncertainty and bewilderment reigned among the lower orders. This explains the many contradictory statements made by the members of Grudge. If most of them did not notice that they were being manipulated from above, Captain Ruppelt at least suspected that something was amiss.

'From above' in this case meant the C.I.A. A name with sinister overtones, perhaps, but the C.I.A. had good reason to be interested in the U.F.O. phenomenon. In order to understand this fateful development better, some of the background must be filled in.

The year 1947 was already significant in the U.F.O. field because of the Arnold sighting. But a far more significant, if less obvious, development in that year was the creation of the C.I.A.

After the end of the Second World War, President Truman had dissolved the existing secret service, the O.S.S. or Office of Strategic Services. His reasoning was that in peace-time there was no longer any necessity for covert political activity, paramilitary operations or psychological tactics. But Truman still saw the necessity for an institution which had the task of collecting, analysing and coordinating information – especially secret information. Thus in 1947 the American President requested Congress to pass the National Security Act which provided for the foundation of the Central Intelligence Agency – the C.I.A.

In the tense atmosphere of the Cold War, the security experts had little difficulty in persuading Congress of its necessity, and the passing of the National Security Act of 1947 gave the C.I.A. special privileges. The new authority was exempted from normal Congressional investigation procedures, and in 1949 the Central Intelligence Act extended its protection even further. The most serious consequences, however, arose from the article included in the Act of 1947 which gave the C.I.A. 'full powers . . . to exercise other functions and duties not directly related to intelligence'.

This short, apparently harmless phrase enabled the C.I.A. to create a secret charter over the years, which on the one hand was in full agreement with the provisions of the National Security Act and was based on the President's own stipulations, but on the other hand almost directly contradicted the clear intention of the law which had created the C.I.A. A few 'insignificant' words passed by Congress had given the C.I.A. the freedom to involve itself in secret affairs which had nothing to do with its basic task. As a result, the C.I.A. was to become the most powerful body in the Western world.

In the middle of the Cold War, U.F.O. sightings were becoming more and more frequent. Was the West being threatened by a new Russian secret weapon? Perhaps a weapon invented by German scientists which had been taken over by the Russians at the end of the war? For some time this explanation seemed the favourite, and was also taken seriously by the C.I.A. An order classified as 'above top secret' went out from the C.I.A. to investigate the origin of the U.F.O.s. As the U.S. military intelligence services are all subordinate to the C.I.A., the latter automatically received all project analyses and reports. It soon transpired that the U.F.O.s were an invention neither of the Russians nor of any other earthly nation – and that the Russians were just as bewildered by the phenomenon as the Americans, since U.F.O.s had appeared in the East as well as in the West.

The final report of Project Sign, which stated that U.F.O.s were extraterrestrial spaceships, faced the C.I.A. with an entirely novel situation and seemed to open up a wealth of unhoped-for opportunities.

What interested the C.I.A. in particular was the prospect that with a little bit of luck they might instantaneously gain possession of an entirely new technology involving revolutionary scientific knowledge. One of these extraterrestrial spaceships, if it could be captured, would be of inestimable value to the United States. But it was equally possible that the Russians would get hold of one first, and this would be a fatal blow to the U.S.A. Thus, for the C.I.A., it was an absolute necessity to be first on the scene if such a possibility should arise. Naturally the Russians were moved by similar considerations. And so the race to catch a U.F.O. began.

The public naturally had to be excluded. A U.F.O. could not just be commandeered from wherever it landed, and, more important, the Russians would probably have to be headed off first. The C.I.A. therefore evolved a plan which involved using the Russian Secret Service as a channel through which to create confusion in the U.S.S.R., while secretly making every effort to investigate the technology and the methods used by the U.F.O.s. Since the interest of the mass media and the public at large was a serious obstacle to secrecy, the C.I.A. (and, as later transpired, the K.G.B.) resorted to explaining away the U.F.O. phenomenon and bringing it into ridicule.

The director of the C.I.A. at the time, Admiral R.H. Hillenkoetter, confirmed many years later that 'The Air Force has constantly misled the public about U.F.O.s.'

This, then, was the reason for the 'evasive tactics' employed by Project Grudge. But it was only the beginning.

In 1955, after the Russians, Americans, Canadians and others had given up their fruitless hunt for U.F.O.s, Secret Service leaders from the U.S.A., the U.S.S.R., France and England met in Geneva. There they unanimously agreed on a policy of strict secrecy over the U.F.O. phenomenon *vis-à-vis* the general public.

The beginning of Project Grudge happened to coincide with the publication of the first outlandish tales of encounters with alien beings. The timing, as far as the C.I.A. and the American Air Force were concerned, could not have been more convenient. Nothing could be more effective in persuading the public that the whole U.F.O. phenomenon was a lot of nonsense.

In 1950 the Aerojet General Corporation put an engineer named Daniel W. Fry in charge of the instrumentation of the missile control systems at the White Sands missile testing ground near Las Cruces in New Mexico. Later Fry played an important part in the development of the guidance system of the Atlas booster rockets used in the moon shots and for a time was an adviser to the California Institute of Technology. From this it would seem reasonable to assume that Fry is a realist, not prone to fantasy. But events were to cast some doubt on the matter.

The following 'close encounter' took place, according to Fry, on 4 July 1950. He had gone for an evening run to the old static V-2 testing ground. It was about a mile and a half to the centre of the ground and on the way Fry had happened to look up at the sky. He noticed that a line of stars was apparently hidden behind something and on closer observation eventually made out an oval object which sank slowly to earth and landed silently about twenty-five yards away from him. All that could be heard was the cracking of branches as it settled.

Fry ran round the object, which he estimated to be twenty-six feet high and thirty feet in diameter. He could not see any joints or windows, and the occupants of the strange object, if there were any, would have had to leave it from the top or the bottom. Fry went nearer and touched the upper surface which seemed to be of polished silvery metal and·gave off a scarcely perceptible violet glow. It felt unbelievably smooth and seemed to be somewhat warmer than the air temperature. Fry tapped it lightly and immediately felt a prickling in his hands and fingers. At the same time a voice which seemed to come from nowhere said: 'Better not touch the hull, pal, it's still hot.'

Fry stumbled backwards in alarm and measured his length on the ground. Later he remembered that he had been amazed by the idiomatic language, which had led him to assume that he was being addressed by an American. But he had scarcely had time to register the thought when the voice said quietly: 'No, I'm not an American like you, but because of my present task I have to act like an American. And the fact that you took me for a fellow-countryman shows that my efforts to learn your language and idioms during the past two years have been successful. I have not yet personally visited your planet. Another four years will have to pass before I can adapt myself to the Earthly atmosphere and gravity, and before I am immune to the germs of your planet. The main aim of our present expedition is to discover just how adaptable man is. We chiefly want to discover whether man is capable of adjusting his mental world to concepts which are far removed from his customary way of thinking. For centuries, our ancestors have been sending expeditions to Earth, but unfortunately they have met with little success. This time we hope to find more fertile ground and more intelligent human beings. For we would like to help the inhabitants of earth with their further development.'

Fry stood in the sand, listening in amazement as the alien voice continued: 'I can imagine that it must be tiring for you to stand there following my discourse. Perhaps you would like to take a little trip. This remote-controlled space capsule is only intended as a transport machine, but there is nevertheless a small passenger cabin with a couple of seats. I myself am in the control centre, the mother ship as it is called on Earth, 900 miles above the globe.'

At this, part of the underside of the hull slid inwards and Fry entered a cabin about nine feet long by seven feet wide. It contained four large, anatomically shaped seats.

The voice addressed Fry again, suggesting a thirty-minute flight to New York and back. Fry agreed in amazement, instinctively clutched his seat and braced his legs. Seconds later, Earth, as he put it, 'fell away beneath me at an unbelievable speed'. He did not feel the slightest acceleration and in his opinion the U.F.O. did not move from the spot, hence the expression that Earth 'fell away'. Shortly after he took off, the lights of Las Cruces appeared in the lower left-hand corner of the door opening, which had become transparent. From this Fry deduced that the craft must have climbed some 10,000 feet in two or three seconds. But he could not understand how he had not felt any acceleration during take-off.

The disembodied voice answered his query with the information that the method of propulsion resembled a gravitational field and acted not only on every atom of the spaceship itself but also on every mass of atoms inside it – including a pilot or passenger. The craft's powers of acceleration were limited only by the power of the propulsion unit. As this energy was proportionally related to the mass, and Earth's gravity acted equally on the craft and its occupant, the force between the seat and his body remained constant. There was only one limitation – the energy grew less to the same extent that Earth's gravity diminished as one got further away from it. On interstellar journeys, therefore, when travelling away from the planets with their gravitational fields, an artificial source of gravity was necessary.

'We are accustomed to a gravity less than half that of Earth,' the voice concluded quietly.

Over New York the U.F.O. descended to 100,000 feet. From what had been an indeterminate sea of light, millions of individual lights came into focus, looking like blueish-white diamonds on a dark background. But his stay over New York was very short, and Fry was flown back to White Sands even faster then he had come.

After landing, he staggered out of the spaceship and ran a few steps across the sand, thoroughly confused by his experience. When he finally looked up, the door of the craft had disappeared again, and with an orange-red glow issuing from around its middle, it suddenly shot vertically upwards into the night sky. Fry was dragged forwards several yards by the vacuum caused by its take-off and almost lost his balance. However, he did not lose sight of the object, and watched as the orange-red glow turned to dark violet before it finally disappeared from view.

It is said that Fry immediately made a written report on his experience, recording all the technical details, but because White Sands was subject to strict security measures as a military base, the report was not published until twelve years later.

Stories of actual contact – the so-called close encounters – are the biggest obstacle to our understanding of U.F.O.s, representing the darker side of an otherwise eminently respectable phenomenon. They led to the creation of a kind of ersatz religion, a proliferation of U.F.O. sects which have brought the whole subject of U.F.O.s into discredit.

But does this necessarily mean that all reports of contact (and they are very numerous) are deliberate fabrications? This would undoubtedly be the easiest view to take and it would solve a lot of problems. For as soon as we accept just one of these close encounters as real, or even admit its possibility, we open up a whole range of unfamiliar perspectives. The problem is that some of these reports do ring remarkably true; but however true they may sound, they remain only reports from second hand, and the fact is that we still have nothing concrete, nothing substantial, nothing that can be definitively proved.

On 7 July 1952, the North American Newspaper Alliance

carried a report of a U.F.O. landing in East Germany. The landing had been witnessed by Oskar Linke, the former mayor of Gleimershausen near Meiningen. Linke made the following statement under oath, in front of English and American investigators:

As I was intending to defect to the West, I often rode to the West German frontier on my motor cycle with my twelve-year-old daughter in the side-car. In this way the Russian frontier officials soon got to know us and were deceived as to our real intentions. One week before our escape, we were riding back to our house in the afternoon from our trip to the frontier. We passed by a small wood which is some five kilometres away from the West German frontier. Suddenly my daughter pointed to something bright shining through the trees. We immediately stopped, hid the motor cycle in the bushes and cautiously crept towards it through the trees. About twenty-five or thirty metres away we then saw a disc-shaped object in a clearing which was perhaps eight metres in diameter. It gave the effect of being illuminated and a square construction projected upwards from the middle, which was dome-shaped on top. This superstructure was darker than the object and was reminiscent of polished aluminium.

We had hidden ourselves behind a small hill and observed two humanoid beings, who were about 1.20 metres high, coming from the other side of the clearing. They were wearing shining silver overalls; one of the two had a box-shaped object which was as large as three cigarette packets, one on top of the other, on his chest; this had a blueish winking light on the front of it. The aliens were walking in single file; the one behind tapped the leader on his transparent helmet; at this, both of them stopped. When one of them suddenly turned towards us, my daughter gave out a suppressed gasp. The aliens immediately ran quickly towards a gap in the square superstructure and disappeared inside the object. It was only now that we noticed two rows of round holes running around the flying object, almost like ship's portholes. The rectangular superstructure slowly disappeared into the dome-like top and the object now lifted off from the ground. A rectangular construction could be seen on the underside; probably this was the propulsion unit. The flying object rose some thirty metres into the air, hovered for a while and then suddenly shot away.

While making his statement, Linke told the English and American officials that he was firmly convinced that he had seen a new type of Russian aircraft. He had never heard of U.F.O.s.

The theory that the U.F.O. sightings, and particularly stories of contact, are a psychological phenomenon, a by-product of increasing alienation in our technological world, seems entirely without foundation. In fact, over the course of the centuries, there have been repeated reports of U.F.O. sightings and also of close encounters.

In 1790, for instance, a French police official named Liabeuf was sent from Paris to Alençon in order to investigate an unusual incident for his superiors. He made the following report:

On 12 June at 5 o'clock in the morning, some peasants had observed an enormous globe, which seemed to be surrounded by flame. At first they thought it must be a Montgolfier balloon which had caught fire. But they were amazed by its great speed and the whistling noise it produced. The globe slowed down, made a rocking motion, and crashed down on a hilltop, uprooting the whole of the surrounding vegetation. The heat given off by the object was so great that bushes and grass caught fire.

The peasants succeeded in stemming the progress of the fire, which would otherwise have destroyed the whole district.

In the evening the globe was still warm. And then an unusual – one might say unbelievable – event took place; it was witnessed by two mayors, a physician and three other local authorities, who confirm my report – not forgetting the dozen peasants who were also present.

The ball, which was large enough to contain a carriage, was completely intact after its crash.

News of the incident soon spread, and driven by curiosity people flocked to the spot from all directions.

Suddenly a door opened and – this is the most interesting part – a person came out, exactly like us but strangely dressed, in clothes which hung close about his body. When this man saw all the people, he murmured something and ran into the undergrowth.

The peasants instinctively drew back in fear, and that saved them, for shortly afterwards the ball exploded noiselessly, fragments flew in all directions and then dissolved into a kind of powder.

A search was made for the mysterious man, but met with no success. He seemed to have disappeared into thin air, for not the slightest trace of him has been discovered. As if he had disappeared from our world.

Was he not of our world, since he appeared in such a strange manner? I am no scholar, but this thought suddenly came into my head.

The report on this incident was sent to the French Academy of Sciences and was received by its celebrated scholars with all the sarcasm which might have been expected of them. They declared categorically that it was impossible for a living being to arrive on Earth in such a manner. They also declined an invitation to visit the site, so that they could see with their own eyes the hole produced by the ball's landing, which remained visible for years afterwards.

A being who fell from the sky – and under the circumstances

described – it was just too much! Hadn't they already had enough trouble with the physicist Ernst Friedrich Chladni? This admittedly brilliant man had stood all the laws of physics on their head and declared that 'stones – meteorites – fall from the sky.' He at any rate had received his just desserts and been showered with scorn and derision. The person worst offended by Chladni's assertion was the famous chemist and member of the Académie Française, Antoine Laurent Lavoisier. 'Stones cannot fall from the sky, since there are no stones in the sky,' was Lavoisier's view.

But Chladni would not give up, and in 1794 he proved that they did fall from the sky, a discovery for which no one was grateful. The scientific establishment continued to ignore the fact for many years to come in the hope that the cosmic stones would somehow go away.

Morris K. Jessup must have felt much the same as Chladni. For him U.F.O.s were extraterrestrial spaceships, even though his colleagues laughed at him and began to avoid him. His studies of historical cases, in which he took a special interest, only strengthened Jessup's conviction that extraterrestrial intelligences have repeatedly visited earth. He also found it significant that people always used the concepts and terminology of their own time in describing the puzzling phenomena which they had witnessed. This was particularly notable in the mass sightings of 1896 and 1897.

4

Those Daring Flying Machines

Around the turn of the century, more exactly in the years 1896 and 1897, thousands of Americans in Texas and California were amazed by the sudden appearance of some strangely glowing flying objects which resembled giant cigars. What made the sightings even more remarkable was the fact that they took place some seven years before the first motorized flight made by the Wright brothers at Kitty Hawk in 1903, and four and a half years before Count Zeppelin astonished the world with the first airship flight over the Baltic, on 2 July 1900.

Over Sacramento, bright, multicoloured lights were seen swinging up and down, while crowds in Oklahoma were amazed to see a vehicle some 160 feet long with rotor-like wings and a gigantic searchlight on its underside which lit up the ground.

But flying objects were not only observed on dry land. Ships' crews at sea saw shining globes or disc-shaped objects which emerged from the water and rose into the air. Strange 'discs' or 'wheels' were often seen off the Chinese and Japanese coasts, but only occasionally in Europe.

In March and April 1897, the reports of sightings in America showed a sudden increase, being concentrated as before on the area between Texas and Michigan. On 25 April 1897 the *Daily Texarkanian*, the daily paper of Texarkana, Arkansas, reported the fantastic experience of Judge Lawrence A. Byrne. This was the story of a man 'known for his truthfulness by his fellow men':

I was down on McKinney bayou Friday looking after the surveying of a tract of land and, in passing through a thicket to an open space, saw a strange-looking object anchored to the ground. On approaching I found it to be the airship I have read so much about of late. It was manned by three men who spoke a foreign language, but judging from their looks, would take them to be Japs. They saw my astonishment and beckoned me to follow them, and on complying, I was shown through the ship.

The judge also stated that the ship was made of aluminium.

Perhaps it was a sign of the times that so-called 'contact witnesses' at this period usually stated that the crew members of the flying objects were men with beards. One of the most amusing contact stories of the year 1897 was published by the Saginaw *Courier-Herald*:

Bell Plains, Iowa, April 16 – The citizens of Linn Grove declare there is no longer any doubt among them of the existence of an airship. Yesterday morning a large object was seen slowly moving in the heavens in a northerly direction and seemed to be making preparations to alight. James Evans, liveryman; F.G. Ellis, harness dealer; Ben Buland, stock dealer; David Evans, and Joe Croskey jumped into a rig and started in pursuit. They found the airship had alighted four miles north of town, and when within 700 yards, it spread its four monstrous wings and flew off toward the north. Its occupants threw out two large boulders of unknown composition, which were taken to the village and are now on exhibition.

There were two queer-looking persons on board, who made desperate attempts to conceal themselves. Evans and Croskey, say they had the longest whiskers they ever saw in their lives. Nearly every citizen in Linn Grove saw the airship as it sailed over the town, and the excitement is intense.

On 15 April, the *Argus-Leader* in Sioux Falls, South Dakota, and a whole series of other newspapers published the following report under the dateline Springfield, Illinois.

Farm workers Adolph Winkle and John Hulle signed affidavits stating that an airship had landed two miles outside Springfield to repair some electrical apparatus on board. The farmhands said they had talked to the occupants of the machine, two men and a woman, and were told it had flown to Springfield from Quincy, about 100 miles away, in half an hour.

Affidavits were also signed on 8 May 1897 by Sheriff J. Sumpter Jr and his deputy John McKenire of Garland County, Arkansas, relating to an experience they had had two days earlier.

While they were patrolling in a northerly direction, they had noticed a light shining high in the sky, which had suddenly disappeared. As the two men were looking for loitering tramps, they avoided speaking out loud, so as not to draw attention to themselves. They rode on through the hills for a while and the light suddenly reappeared, much nearer to the ground than before. The lawmen stopped their horses and watched as it sank further and further, finally disappearing behind a hill. They rode on again, about half a mile towards the hill, until their horses suddenly shied and refused to go any further. The lawmen now noticed two figures carrying lights, about forty yards away. They immediately shouldered their Winchester rifles and called out: 'Who is that, and what are you doing?'

A small bearded man came forward with a lamp in his hand and when questioned informed the sheriff and his deputy that he was on a journey in an airship with a young man and woman. The lawmen clearly saw the outline of a cigar-shaped object about 600 feet long, which looked exactly like a sketch of a flying object which had recently appeared in the newspapers. They asked the strangers why the blinding light on the airship was continually being turned on and off, and were told that it was a means of saving propulsive energy. As the lawmen had to finish their patrol, they rode away. When they came back about forty minutes later, there was no one there. They had seen and heard nothing as the craft took off and left the area.

One hypothesis, which might explain these sightings, is that an inventor was secretly testing some new invention, though if such were the case one wonders what happened to them both. If this were so, the inventor would have to have been in advance of Count Zeppelin, whose first rigid airship – the LZ 1 – did not fly until several years later. This craft was 420 feet long, equipped with two Daimler engines of fifteen horse-power each, which gave it a maximum speed of 20.25 m.p.h. It is highly probable that airship designs were published in newspapers several years beforehand, but it should not be forgotten that the first Zeppelin was a primitive craft in comparison with the flying objects as they were described by those who saw them.

Everything seems to indicate that something was actually seen in 1897. Even allowing for the extent to which observers' imaginations must have been stimulated by reading newspaper articles, there are remarkable similarities between the different reports from all over America, all of which described an object far in advance of its time. The same features appeared over and over again – cigar-shaped objects in aluminium or similar metal with propulsion units; the hovering, vertical take-offs and high speeds; the brightly shining lights.

Moreover, if one plots the geographical location and timing of these sightings on a map, it soon becomes clear that they represent a dead straight flight-path over long distances.

Perhaps I have so far given the impression that mass sightings of U.F.O.s are a purely American phenomenon, but this is not the case.

At the beginning of the 1930s, large, grey flying machines without nationality markings or other insignia appeared over Europe, and particularly Scandinavia. They frequently appeared during heavy storms, moving over towns, railways, military complexes and ships at sea, and very often turned off their engines. Many of the reports spoke of gigantic four-engined machines. One group of five witnesses claimed to have seen a gigantic aeroplane with eight propellers. But at that time there were practically no private aircraft in Scandinavia, and large airliners were only in the early stages of development. In 1926, Admiral Byrd and Floyd Bennet had flown from Spitzbergen in Norway to the North Pole in a three-engine Fokker. This flight aroused a great deal of public attention in Scandinavia at the time, and photos of the aircraft appeared repeatedly in the press. When the mysterious flying machines appeared six years later in the Scandinavian sky, many witnesses compared them with Byrd's three-engine Fokker.

The Swedish Air Force, at least, took these reports seriously. In 1934 they sent twenty-four biplanes to a remote area in search of the 'ghost fliers' that had been reported there. An exhaustive search by land, sea and air was carried out in an effort to trace the phenomenon. The Swedish Air Force pilots had to operate under perilous conditions, and two machines crashed during the search.

At Piteå in northern Sweden on 22 January 1934, the curate of Langtrask reported that during the last two years, he had repeatedly seen strange flying machines in this district. These were the so-called 'ghost fliers', twelve of which had flown over his community the previous summer, one after the other and always in the same direction, from south-west to north-east. Although the machines had flown very low on four different occasions, neither national insignia nor other markings had been visible. But when one of them had flown directly over the rectory, three people had appeared briefly in the cockpit. The curate added that the machines were grey and had only one wing on either side.

Up till December 1933 this phenomenon had scarcely been mentioned in the press. One of the first reports appeared on 24 December 1933, in Kalix. It stated that on Christmas Eve, at about 6 o'clock in the evening, a mysterious flying object had appeared from the direction of Bottensea, flown over Kalix and disappeared in a westerly direction. The area was flooded with light which came from the machine.

On 27 December 1933 the *New York Times* devoted an extensive article to a mysterious flying object which had circled directly over New York with a thunderous noise, during a terrible blizzard.

According to the article, at 9.30 on the morning of 26 December, the noise of an aircraft circling in the middle of the snowstorm had been heard all over Manhattan. After a newsreader had made the event public, telephone reports began pouring in from all directions. The *New York Times* stated: 'After checking the different calls, it must be assumed that the flier advanced as far as 72nd Street, circled over Central Park and then flew on towards 23rd Street and as far as the Bronx.'

After that, all was quiet until 2.25. Then the noise of engines was heard again over Riverside Drive and 155th Street.

Every airfield in the Metropolitan District announced that all flights had been cancelled during the day because of the weather, and also there had been no emergency landings by aircraft lost in the storm.

In 1933 aircraft were not yet capable of flying in very bad weather. There was no existing aircraft type which could stay in the air during a five- or six-hour blizzard. Yet the machine which was heard over New York obviously was able to do so. It was never identified.

On 4 February 1934 the London correspondent of the *New York Times* reported on a similar phenomenon which had occurred over London.

Then shortly after Christmas, another 'ghost aeroplane' appeared in Scandinavia. It was observed both in Norway and Sweden as it flew to and fro across the frontier. Similar reports were received from the Swedish town of Tärnaby and from Langmo Vefsn in Norway. On 28 December, the Swedish 4th Flying Corps was sent to Tärnaby to investigate.

On 10 January a crowd of people in Tärnaby observed a shining light at a height of about 1,200 feet, which turned and flew away towards Archeplog. About a quarter of an hour later, inhabitants of this town heard noises in the air. They ran out into the open to look. The light subsequently appeared over Rortrask, north-east of Norsjö. Eyewitnesses maintained that the engines had cut out three times while the machine was directly over them. It had flown so low that the whole area was bathed in light.

On the same day, two landings by 'ghost fliers' were reported at Trondheim in Norway.

On the previous Wednesday evening a machine had landed near the island of Gyeslingen, outside Rørvik, and another at Kvaloy in the district of Naniudal, both in the remote north of Norway. From Gyeslingen came a report that observers had seen a blinding ray of light and heard a loud noise of engines. The machine had then landed on the water and stayed there for an hour and a half. After the landing the light had gone out.

The Norwegian cruiser *Adler* was immediately sent to the

district, but by the time it arrived the flying object had already gone. Reports of sightings frequently spoke of blinding white lights, and the comparison with a searchlight repeatedly appeared.

In February 1934, alarmed by the constant reports of ghost aeroplanes, the defence ministries of Sweden, Norway and Finland, decided to carry out a thorough investigation of the areas affected. It was obvious from the reports that it was not one or two aircraft, but a whole series of them which were violating the airspace of these countries. Most of the machines were larger than any known military aircraft and were apparently able to operate under the most difficult weather conditions and over dangerous mountain terrain. According to the military, this could only have been achieved with the help of properly organized bases providing the necessary ground staff, spare parts and fuel. But despite the combined efforts of the three countries' military forces, no such bases were found.

On 30 April 1934, the Swedish Major-General Reutersward made the following statement to the press:

It is obvious from a comparison of these reports that illegal air traffic is taking place over our military restricted areas.

Many reports have been received from reliable persons who have closely observed these mysterious fliers. And the same observation is made repeatedly: the machines possessed no national insignia or identification marks. It is impossible to explain away the whole phenomenon as imagination. The question is, who are they and why have they penetrated our airspace?

For two years, all was quiet, but in 1936 the U.F.O.s reappeared in Scandinavia, using the same route they had taken in 1934. Coming from the far north, they passed in a southerly direction over northern Norway, then diagonally across Sweden and back again.

After the Second World War, the sightings continued. On 10 June 1946 some U.F.O.s were seen over Finland which were similar to the German V-bombs. And over a period of some weeks, thousands of people throughout Norway and Sweden saw lights, cigar-shaped objects, and unidentified flying machines with wings. The most frequent sightings were in the sparsely populated far north. The European press made a meal of the incidents and the 'ghost fliers' of the 1930s now became 'ghost missiles'. These U.F.O.s were eventually observed all over Europe, from the far north to Greece. They appeared on radar screens, were photographed, and their recorded speeds ranged from 400 to 1,000 m.p.h.

British and Scandinavian newspapers accused the Russians of testing new military missiles in Northern Europe, which Moscow, of course, promptly denied.

In September, a 'green fireball' was seen over Portugal, and a projectile flew over Casablanca trailing fire. Oslo was visited by 'great glowing things' which fell from the sky and exploded with a deafening noise.

The Swedish government was so disturbed by the sightings of 'ghost missiles' that it turned to the American government for help. They responded by sending the Army's chief of intelligence, General James A. Doolittle, to investigate the phenomenon on the spot. Although he was able to explain away many of the sightings, there still remained more than twenty per cent for which he could find no justification.

Jessup naturally possessed detailed information on all these sightings, and he came to the conclusion that after excluding all possible mistakes and misinterpretations there remained a solid core of sightings which represented the actual U.F.O. problem. One notable feature which emerged was that whereas in the balloon age at the end of the eighteenth century, there were reports of 'balls' in the sky, at the end of the nineteenth century, i.e. a few years before the first flights by a Zeppelin and motorized aircraft, there were reports of mysterious motorized airships, with or without wings. Then in the 1930s came 'multi-engined ghost aircraft', and after the end of the Second World War the apparitions changed to mysterious 'missiles'. With man's first steps into space the classic disc shape reappeared. Discs and cigar-shaped objects seem to have always been the subject of sightings.

From these different forms taken by the sightings, Jessup evolved the theory that these extraterrestrial visitors are able to adapt their flying machines to the circumstances and concepts of each different period.

The American writer and U.F.O. researcher, John A. Keel, goes a step further and suggests that U.F.O.s and their crews are visitors from an alien, possibly psychic, dimension. Being independent of our material world, they can manipulate the form of their machines at will.

Keel's thesis, which he puts forward in his book, *U.F.O.s: Operation Trojan Horse*, can be summed up as follows: U.F.O.s do not appear to exist as tangible fabricated objects. They do not conform to the natural laws with which we are familiar. They seem only to be metamorphoses, transformations which are able to adapt themselves to the capacities of our intelligence. Thousands of contacts with these beings lead us to the conclusion that they are deliberately making fools of us.

Keel's theory is hard to accept, since it relegates the phenomenon to the sphere of the supernatural, the world of demons and dark doings and of medieval superstition. Equally difficult to accept is the pet theory of U.F.O. cultists, that a 'world space brotherhood' has resolved to save humanity from its misery and is constantly paying us visits to see how we are getting on. Yet these 'visits' do seem to be a recurrent and persistent phenomenon.

On 4 April 1950, President Truman held a press conference at Key West, Florida, in the course of which he stated that U.F.O.s originated neither in the U.S.A. nor in any other terrestrial nation. The conference was prompted by an invasion of flying saucers on 17 March 1950, on a scale unprecedented in the United States. More than five hundred silvery disc-shaped objects had flown over the nuclear restricted area in New Mexico, noiselessly and at incredible speed. They were observed on three successive days between 11 a.m. and 1 p.m. over the town of Farmington, in the north of New Mexico. The sightings were extensively reported in the local press. The *Farmington Times* of 18 March, for example, reported under the headline 'U.F.O. fleet over Farmington' that 50,000 inhabitants of the town had seen strange flying objects in the sky on the previous day, adding that whatever else they may have been, they certainly caused a major sensation in the town.

The official Air Force report on the Farmington sighting described them as 'particles of cotton floating in the air', regardless of the fact that the area is quite unsuitable for cotton cultivation.

The case was problematical enough for the staff of Project Grudge, but worse was to come.

5

Cat and Mouse Games

In the night of 19/20 July 1952, some unidentified flying objects threw the air traffic controllers of the American capital into a state of uproar. At about 11.40 p.m. a group of U.F.O.s had erupted on to the radar screens of the civil air control centre of Washington National Airport, at first travelling slowly, at no more than 100 to 125 m.p.h., but then shooting away at a fantastic speed.

At the same time the crews of several different airliners reported seeing mysterious lights which crossed their flight-paths at varying speeds. Their reports were confirmed by others from eyewitnesses on the ground.

Pilots Harry Barnes, Ed Nugent, Jim Ritchey and James Copeland did not trust their eyes, and decided to check. They contacted the control tower and heard from the radar operator, Howard Cockelin, that the same objects were visible on his screen.

'I can even see one with the naked eye – I've no idea what it is,' he said.

The four airline pilots followed the U.F.O.s for a while on their screens, then Ritchey noticed that one of them was trailing an airliner which had just taken off. He immediately informed the captain, an experienced pilot named Pireman, and gave him the U.F.O.s' position. Then suddenly, all trace of the U.F.O.s had been wiped from the radar screens. The pilots were dumbfounded.

At the same moment, Pireman came on the air and said that he had seen the object, but before he had been able to approach it, it had suddenly shot upwards and disappeared in a matter of seconds. When the U.F.O. formation reappeared a little later, chief radar controller Harry Barnes became alarmed and contacted the Air Force High Command, who finally sent up two F-94 interceptors to investigate at around 3 o'clock in the morning.

A squadron of interceptors was normally stationed at Bolling Air Force base, a couple of miles away, to defend the White House and the Capitol. But the squadron had secretly been transferred to New Castle County Airport in Wilmington, Delaware, a hundred miles away, since the runway at Bolling was in need of repair. It took the fighters half an hour to cover this distance, and when they had arrived over Washington they were directed towards the U.F.O.s by the airline pilots. As soon as the fighters approached, however, the U.F.O.s vanished, thwarting all attempts at visual contact as if they had followed the radio dialogue between the fighter pilots and the control tower. At the same time, eyewitnesses on the ground reported strange 'lights' manoeuvering individually in the sky. Two of the U.F.O.s had meanwhile broken away and were flying down the restricted corridor over the White House, while a third circled over the Capitol.

In the course of the night, U.F.O.s appeared again and again on the radar screens. One of the objects was even sighted simultaneously by the three radar stations at National Airport and the Maryland Air Force base, three miles north of Washington. But the same thing happened as before. As soon as the jet fighters appeared, the U.F.O.s vanished from the scene, and from the radar screens.

The first reports came from Newport News in Virginia, where

the U.F.O.s took the form of bright rotating lights of varying colours. When another strange light was seen in the sky a few minutes later from the Langley Field air base in Virginia, another jet fighter was sent up to look. The control tower guided it towards the U.F.O. until the pilot had it in view, but it disappeared as soon as the interceptor drew near, 'just as if someone had switched the light off'. The pilot had a radar bearing and was able to follow the object which was now invisible to him for a few minutes. After he had landed again at Langley Field, the objects reappeared over Washington, and again fighters were sent up to intercept them.

This time, however, the U.F.O.s made no attempt to disappear and a regular cat and mouse game ensued. Each time the fighters came close enough to get a good look at the flying objects, they shot away at a fantastic speed, going just far enough to prevent their being seen well. While this was going on, one of the pilots suddenly noticed that he was completely surrounded by U.F.O.s. He nervously called up the control tower to ask what he should do, but before the tower had time to reply, the U.F.O.s had already drawn back and left him alone. After half an hour of fruitless pursuit, the fighters had to give up and return to base, as they were running out of fuel.

This particular series of sightings made international headlines; the public was in uproar, and an official denial was needed to restore general calm. But no one could explain the phenomenon itself, and enquiries poured into the Pentagon, including one from President Truman himself.

This particular incident was specially significant since the observations of eyewitnesses on the ground and in the air, and the radar pictures, all agreed with one another. Even the colour of the flying objects was generally described as changing from orange to green to red. In the face of public pressure, the Air Force finally decided that something must be done.

The Chief of Staff, Lieutenant General Nathan Twining, decided to hold a press conference, with the aim of calming public fears and putting an end to rumour. The conference took place on 29 July 1952 and was the longest the Air Force had held since the Second World War. The speakers included Major General John A. Samford, Director of Air Force Intelligence, Major General Roger A. Ramey, Chief of the Air Defense Command, and Captain E.J. Ruppelt from Project Blue Book.

Samford opened the conference on a note of noncommittal amiability, announcing that the Air Force was more or less convinced that the radar sightings of the past two weeks were caused by temperature inversions in the atmosphere. The radar installations had picked up the reflections of lights from the ground which had bounced off a layer of cold air trapped between two warm ones – the so-called temperature inversions.

On closer questioning, the reporters received evasive, empty answers. Samford stated the Air Force's intention of employing an independent scientist to carry out an intensive investigation of the Washington sightings. (In the event it went no further than the intention.)

When the reporters argued that a number of airline pilots had actually seen the objects, Samford was only able to answer lamely that the Air Force had no explanation to offer. He tried to justify himself with the sweeping assertion that so far no astronomer had actually seen a U.F.O. – a statement which by no means coincided with the facts.

In fact, Samford should have been better informed. Surely he must have known of the U.F.O. sightings made by his distinguished compatriot, Professor Clyde Tombaugh, the astronomer who had discovered the planet Pluto in 1930 and had for a time been adviser to the U.S. government on space questions.

Tombaugh sighted a U.F.O. on the evening of 10 August

1949 from the terrace of his house in Las Cruces, New Mexico. Around 10.45 p.m. he had observed a dark, cigar-shaped object against the sky. He had noticed at least one row of shining hatch-like openings running from the middle towards the back. He later stated that they could also have been square windows.

But this is a digression.

To return to the press conference, Samford further announced to the press that the Air Force had received a number of reports on U.F.O.s, 'from believable observers about relatively un-believable things'. These formed some twenty per cent of all reports. Finally Samford laid particular emphasis on the obser-vation that U.F.O.s in no way represented a threat to national security. This was a somewhat paradoxical statement in view of the fact that in the night before the press conference information had filtered through that Air Force pilots had recently received orders to fire on U.F.O.s if they refused to land. This made nonsense of Samford's explanation about temperature inver-sions. Was he perhaps in possession of 'new scientific knowledge' according to which temperature inversions appeared in military formations and could be shot down or forced to land? If such was the case, he would also have to explain why interceptors had been given the order to pursue a 'meteorological phenomenon'.

No explanation was provided of why experienced radar technicians should have chosen to confuse temperature inver-sions with extraterrestrial spaceships on the occasion of the Washington sighting alone. Neither before nor after the events over Washington did they make such a mistake. They themselves protested at the idea, and moreover, according to radar measurements of the U.F.O.s' speed, they had accelerated from approximately 100 to 7,000 m.p.h. in a few seconds. The wind speed at the time was no more than 20 m.p.h.

The public were also unaware that the U.F.O. sightings over Washington were not the only ones at that time. Nor did

Samford make any mention of it at the press conference, which was packed with some fifty journalists.

One Secret Service report, for instance, shows that on 23 July, luminous bluish-green objects were seen over Boston, and traced by radar. An F-94 pilot who was sent up to investigate reported making visual contact with the U.F.O.s shortly after take-off, but he was outmanoeuvered by their rapid acceleration.

On 28 July, a private individual, George Stock, even managed to get seven snapshots of a disc-shaped object which swept over his house as he was working in the garden. He called his father, who also saw the strange object. During the same period C.I.A. officials confirmed a series of sightings over aircraft factories on the West Coast. Engineers at one of the factories, who observed the manoeuvres of the disc-shaped objects, said that they were undoubtedly machines guided by intelligent minds.

The sightings brought a new wave of public anxiety. What was happening? Where were the U.F.O.s coming from? Had the Russians perhaps developed a new secret weapon?

6

Gru-Fo

The Russians had not developed a new secret weapon. They had serious problems of their own with U.F.O.s, and were wondering if they did not conceal some new American secret weapon. Valentin Akkuratov, a famous Russian pilot, reported having encountered a lens-shaped, pearl-coloured U.F.O. 'with undulating edges' while on a strategic mission in a TU-4 over Greenland.

At first he and his crew thought it must be a new American aircraft type and took cover in the clouds. When they emerged from the clouds a little later they were amazed to find the strange object alongside their own machine. Akkuratov decided to take a closer look and suddenly changed course to take him nearer to the object, at the same time requesting permission from the Aderma air base for the manoeuvre. As soon as Akkuratov had completed his change of course, the U.F.O. made the same manoeuvre and adopted a parallel course to the TU-4. After flying alongside for a quarter of an hour, it again changed its course, moved in front of the TU-4 and suddenly shot up at a steep angle and disappeared.

The Russian crew could make out neither antennae, wings nor windows on the U.F.O., and could not make any guesses about its means of propulsion. Akkuratov merely commented on the 'impossible speed' with which the object had moved away.

He also stated that he had often seen U.F.O.s on his flights over the Baltic, as well as over Murmansk, Kharkov and Gorki.

The Russians not only tried to unravel the secret of the U.F.O. through airborne encounters, they even tried to shoot them down, notably in the hills of Rybinsk, ninety-five miles north of Moscow. The sighting of U.F.O.s there was unfortunate, since the area contained missile sites which formed part of the defence of the Soviet capital. When the U.F.O.s appeared a nervous battery commander panicked and gave an unauthorized order to fire on the gigantic disc. The missiles were fired, but all of them exploded about a mile and a quarter from the target. A second salvo followed, with the same result; there was no third salvo, for in the meantime a number of smaller saucers had gone into action and put the entire electrical system of the missile base out of action. It seemed probable that they had blanketed the circuits with strong electromagnetic fields, for as soon as they withdrew to the mother U.F.O., the electricity began functioning again.

The Romanian, Ion Hobana, science editor of the Bucharest daily paper *Scinteia*, summarized the U.F.O. problem in the Soviet Union as follows:

1. The modern U.F.O. era in Russia began in the year 1946.
2. U.F.O.s in Russia have the same distinguishing characteristics as those in other parts of the world.
3. Although U.F.O. sightings are not published through the mass media, there nevertheless exists a two-way flow of information and reaction between the observers and the public.
4. The *official* attitude to the U.F.O. problem in the Soviet Union is generally speaking as noncommittal as in the West.
5. Nevertheless it is accepted in Russia that the U.F.O.s are

an extraterrestrial phenomenon. This possibility is taken
more seriously in the East than in the West, even in
scientific circles.

It is a little known fact that the number of sightings in the Soviet
Union is enormously large. However, the ordinary Soviet
citizen does not usually bother to report them if only because of
the enormous amount of bureaucratic paperwork involved. The
Soviet Air Force only files reports of sightings by pilots.

'But despite the relatively small number of official reports of
sightings, I believe that U.F.O.s are sighted as often in the East
as in the West', says Hobana.

According to one report, a doctor near the town of Irkutsk
photographed a disc-shaped object from the window of her
laboratory as it landed on four legs.

In the summer of 1952 a gigantic cigar-shaped object at least
2,500 feet long appeared over the town of Voronezh. It slowly
came down to an altitude of some 6,500 feet, where it remained
motionless for a long time. Thousands of people, seeing the
object in broad daylight, were thrown into panic. Then,
suddenly, it vanished. Shortly afterwards a couple of fighter
planes appeared, obviously looking for the U.F.O. Seconds after
they had flown off in bewilderment, the mysterious object
reappeared over the town in the very place it had disappeared
from. A mighty orange-coloured ray shot out of the back of it
and the 'cigar' rose almost vertically in the sky and disappeared
at a fantastic speed.

In a factory producing heavy armaments (the place and exact
date were kept a secret), a mysterious explosion almost
precipitated an international crisis, as the Russians seemed
inclined to put it down to sabotage by American agents. In fact,
it was caused by several cigar- and disc-shaped flying objects,
which had been sighted a week earlier in the neighbourhood of
the factory site. Various eyewitnesses described how they saw a
fireball descend on the factory at daybreak, and this was then

followed by a loud explosion, which was accompanied by 'myriads of brightly shining small globes'. They lit up the whole area in the early morning light and a strong shock-wave was felt by observers. For a few minutes the whole site was covered in a cloud of dust and debris, and when this had cleared, there was nothing left but a crater filled with rubble, where a few minutes previously there had been a section of the factory devoted to the production of missile firing devices.

After the explosion a disc was seen to hover over the site for some time, as if it wanted to be sure that the job had been properly done. When a couple of fighter aircraft appeared, however, it flew off at high speed.

The biggest puzzle for all concerned was the fact that no one had been injured. The factory siren had gone off in warning a few minutes before the explosion and all the workers had taken cover. In the ensuing investigation, however, it turned out that no one had pressed the alarm button – the switch, when inspected, was still in the off position.

The Russians were as mystified by the U.F.O. phenomenon as the Americans. The C.I.A. had this directly from the G.R.U., the Russian military intelligence service, for Lieutenant General Yuri Popov of the G.R.U. was a C.I.A. agent, although the Russians did not discover this until 1958.

As early as 1952, a secret G.R.U. directive (UZ-II/14) ordered an immediate investigation of the U.F.O. problem and contained the following instructions:

Section 3 . . . it is urgently ordered to discover whether the unidentified flying objects are:

(a) secret vehicles of foreign powers which are penetrating Soviet airspace;
(b) misinformative activity by imperialistic secret services;
(c) manned or unmanned extraterrestrial probes engaged in the investigation of Earth; or
(d) an unknown natural phenomenon.

Evidently, there was no doubt in the Soviet Union about the reality of the phenomenon, and secretly, the Russians very soon came to the conclusion that U.F.O.s must be of extraterrestrial origin.

Unfortunately we know very little about the earlier sightings in the Soviet Union. There were numerous ones during the 1950s, but the few reports which leaked through to the West mostly lacked precise details such as names, places and dates, as these were kept secret. The occurrence at the armaments factory, with its overtones of a vengeful hand from the heavens, seems almost too good to be true. However, there were evidently enough disturbingly authentic cases in the Soviet Union for official measures to be taken, and even at this early date the Russians seemed to have arrived at similar conclusions to those reached by the Americans.

Few historical cases were recorded in Russia, but the following report appeared in 1842 in the archives of the Archaeological Commission in St Petersburg:

August 1663
To his Highness the Archimandrite Nikita,
To his Highness the Starosta Matvei,
To his Highness the Starosta Pavel,
To their Highnesses the Starostas of the Synod of the Monastery of St Cyril

First, greetings to the high and well-born lords from their respectful servant Ivachko Ryevskoi.

The kulak Levka Fedorov living in the village of Mys has sent me the following eyewitness account:

According to this the faithful of Belosero went in large numbers to church at Robasero on the fifteenth day of August in the year of the Lord 1663, a Saturday.

And while they were there they heard a loud roaring from the heavens, and many of them left the house of God and assembled outside in the church square. The aforementioned farmer Levka Fedorov was amongst them and saw what happened. For him it was a sign from God. At about the time that midday sounded, a large fireball came down on Roberoso, not from a cloud but from the clearest of all skies. It came from the direction which brings us winter and passed over the church towards the lake. On each side was a band of fire some 150 yards wide and in front two penetrating beams of rays of the same length. Suddenly it disappeared, but when the time had advanced by about an hour, it reappeared over the lake in the same place where it had previously disappeared. When it disappeared from the south towards the west, it passed at a distance of about 1500 yards. But when it then returned again it filled everyone with great fear when it moved westwards and remained for an hour and a half over Robosero. There were fishermen in their boats on the lake about a mile away and they were badly burned by the heat. The water of the lake was lit up to its farthest depths and the fish fled towards the bank. Under the lights the water looked as if it were covered with rust.

A U.F.O. incident reported in the Soviet Union over three hundred years later sounds rather less picturesque in the prosaic language of the twentieth century: 'When U.F.O.s appeared in the spring of 1959 over the control centre of a strategic missile base at Sverdlovsk, they caused widespread panic among radar and Air Force staff.'

7

Orders to Capture

Ten years before this Russian sighting, in 1949, a U.F.O. was sighted over the American missile-testing range at White Sands in New Mexico. A team of scientists under the leadership of Naval Commander R.B. McLaughlin was working in White Sands at the time.

At around 10.30 on the morning of 24 April, the scientists under McLaughlin were preparing for the launching of a gigantic Naval skyhook balloon with a diameter of over a hundred feet. The sky was crystal clear and a weather balloon had already been sent up to test the winds in the upper atmosphere. Part of the scientific team were following the course of the balloon at a height of 11,500 feet when one of the men suddenly called their attention to a second object, much higher in the sky and to the left of it. To their great amazement the scientists saw a silver-white, ellipsoidal U.F.O. One of the scientists swung round the theodolite trained on the weather balloon, fixed it on the U.F.O. and followed its progress for all of a minute. Finally the U.F.O. rose up and disappeared from sight within seconds. With the help of the theodolite, the scientists estimated the object's flying height at fifty miles and its speed at 27,000 m.p.h.

In his report, Commander McLaughlin wrote that he was convinced that the object in question was a U.F.O. and moreover that these saucers are spaceships from other worlds, which are guided by living intelligences.

The military published McLaughlin's statement without restriction – perhaps in error. But there was a sequel to the incident – Commander McLaughlin was unexpectedly transferred from White Sands to the destroyer *Bristol*.

On 10 September 1951 a dramatic occurrence took place in America, which brought about the end of Project Grudge. The pilot and passenger of a T-33, one of them an Air Force Major, observed a flying object between thirty-five and fifty feet in diameter over Fort Monmouth in New Jersey. It swept beneath the aircraft and was described by the witnesses as round, silver-coloured and non-reflecting. The pilot dived in an attempt to detain the U.F.O., but was unsuccessful. The U.F.O. remained beneath the T-33 for a short while, then embarked on a southerly course, veered through 120 degrees and flew off towards the sea.

At exactly the same time an operator of the Army Signal Corps radar centre was demonstrating the radar installation to a group of officers who were visiting the fort. He followed an unidentified object on the radar screen as it moved away at a speed of 500 to 700 m.p.h. but soon lost sight of it because of its speed and erratic course.

On the next day U.F.O.s again showed up on the radar screens at Fort Monmouth, behaving in the same way as on the previous day. This time it was not just a single visit; the objects came and went repeatedly, but moved so quickly that the radar operator was unable to follow them.

These sightings caused a sensation in Fort Monmouth. A number of Air Force officers had even observed them with the naked eye as well as on the radar screen. The radar operator was beside himself and submitted a written request for an explanation of the affair. A copy of his memorandum went to the director of Air Force intelligence, Major General C.B. Cabell, who immediately demanded more detailed information about the Air Force's U.F.O. project. He sent Lieutenant Jerry Cummings (leader of Project Grudge) and his superior, Lieutenant Colonel N.R. Rosengarten (chief of the aircraft and missile division of A.T.I.C.) to Fort Monmouth to investigate.

Cummings and Rosengarten concluded their investigation, with the official explanation that the objects observed had been balloons and false radar echoes, caused by unusual atmospheric conditions. At the same time, Cummings put Cabell in the picture about Project Grudge, and pointed out its weaknesses to him. Cabell also learned that Project Grudge was running out of serious reports of sightings. The whole perspective of the U.F.O. problem prompted Cabell to order the A.T.I.C. to begin a new U.F.O. research project.

The leader of this new project was Air Force Captain Edward J. Ruppelt, who had been highly decorated in the Second World War.

David M. Jacobs, Professor of History at Temple University in Philadelphia, had made a particularly thorough investigation of the background to the Air Force's U.F.O. projects, and on the basis of his findings the Air Force decided to put more funds into Project Grudge and reorganize it. Ruppelt's fundamental reorganization of the project and an increase in sightings in the first months of 1952 prompted the Air Force to dissolve Project Grudge as such and turn it into a self-sufficient organization.

Simultaneously with its change of status, the project received a new name. From now on it was known as Project Blue Book, and Ruppelt, as its leader, received further support from the A.T.I.C. sections specializing in electronics, data analysis, radar and reconnaissance, which were to work directly for Blue Book. Also, the Battelle Memorial Institute in Columbus, Ohio, was commissioned by A.T.I.C. to carry out statistical studies, in particular questionnaires. The results of this work were submitted to the Air Force in May 1953 under the title Project Blue Book, Special Report No. 14.

During this period, Joseph Kaplan, a physicist at California University in Los Angeles and a member of the Air Force's scientific advisory committee, visited Project Blue Book at the Wright-Patterson Air Force base in Dayton, Ohio, where it was stationed. Kaplan was convinced that exact measurements of U.F.O.s were absolutely necessary, but hitherto there had been no way of carrying them out. He therefore proposed to make an analysis of the colour spectrum of U.F.O.s by means of a special diffraction grid, which would enable them to be compared in the laboratory with the spectral lines of known objects such as stars, planets and meteors.

The A.T.I.C. and Blue Book enthusiastically adopted this proposal. And in the course of the year 1952 all possible diffraction grids and cameras were tested for their suitability under the widest possible range of conditions. While Kaplan's plan was still at the development stage, Ruppelt made use of radar pictures at Cabell's suggestion, having contacted the Air Defense Command, which owned some thirty radar screen cameras within the United States. Ruppelt himself briefed the commanding officers for their specialist task. The Air Force Defense Committee was also informed and asked for its consent to the proposed use of radar screen cameras. Ruppelt also included scientists from the Cambridge Research Laboratory, who were already acting in an advisory capacity to the Air Force, in the new programme. It was they who recommended the installation of automatic acoustic receiving devices in areas of intense U.F.O. activity.

Since the Pentagon also wished to be kept informed about the activities of Project Blue Book, Major Dewey Fournet was appointed liaison officer. (Years later Fournet said that the Air Force had deliberately withheld information about U.F.O.s and reports of sightings.) In this capacity, Fournet was a party to all the important developments, investigations and decisions which took place during 1952 and was the most important source of information on Blue Book for the Pentagon.

In the course of time, the Air Force not only granted Ruppelt more and more powers for the project but also carried out the changes he suggested in the investigation of U.F.O. reports. Thus Air Force Ordinance No. 200-5 of 5 April 1952 ordered all intelligence officers in Air Force bases throughout the world to , telegraph reports of sightings directly to the A.T.I.C. and all Air Force control centres in the first instance, and to follow this up by sending extensive written reports by post to the A.T.I.C. Copies of these reports were also received by the chief of Air Force intelligence in Washington. The new Air Force directive even allowed anyone involved in Blue Book to contact any Air Force base directly without going through channels. This new system meant that the A.T.I.C. received all U.F.O. reports as quickly as possible, and Blue Book had more power than any previous project. Intelligence officers were directed to channel all reports of sightings to Blue Book, and the personnel of Blue Book were free to decide for themselves which cases were to be investigated.

Obviously a fictitious, imaginary phenomenon would scarcely have been the subject of so much attention. The C.I.A. was as well aware as anyone that U.F.O.s were real. And they wanted to be sure that they were as up to date on the subject as the K.G.B.

The extent to which the whole U.F.O. field was overrun by the intelligence services is obvious from J.A.N.A.P. (Joint Army Navy Air Force Publication) 146 (B) of September 1951 and December 1953. In this the members of the armed forces and pilots of civil airlines are threatened with a fine of 10,000 dollars and up to ten years in jail for publishing a U.F.O. report. In Air Force Ordinance 200-2 (later renumbered 80-17), it is stated that only false statements and fictitious U.F.O. reports may be published. All real reports should be treated as secret and forwarded to the appropriate authority.

All material evidence had to be forwarded immediately, by air if possible, to the A.T.I.C. in Dayton. This included items such as:

1. Fragments of unidentified flying objects which were definitely from U.F.O.s or could be from them.
2. Radar photographs revealing the flight manoeuvres and speed of flying saucers.
3. Authentic photos of flying saucers.

It was unfortunate for the U.S. Air Force and the C.I.A. that there were exceptionally large numbers of convincing sightings during the 1950s. The public began to suspect that something was amiss in the official treatment of the subject. The staff of Blue Book had their hands full playing down the U.F.O. problem, and there were some cases which it must have found difficult to cope with.

On 20 January 1951, for example, Captain Lawrence W. Vinther of Mid Continent Airlines was asked by the control tower of Sioux City Airport to investigate a 'very bright light' over the airfield. Vinther, together with his co-pilot F. Bachmaier, took his DC-3 towards the light, which suddenly dived headlong on to their machine, overtook it noiselessly and then flew past at high speed some 200 feet above the nose of the DC-3. Both pilots craned round to see where the object had gone to, and discovered that it must have made a 180 degree turn in a. matter of seconds, since it was now flying about 200 feet away on a parallel course with the DC-3 in the same direction. It was a bright, moonlit night, and both pilots were able to get a proper view of the U.F.O. It was the size of a B-29, possibly a little larger, and was cigar-shaped.

The white light seemed to come from a recess in the object's tail. After a few seconds, it lost height, flew past beneath the

airliner and disappeared. An air traffic official who was travelling as a passenger in the DC-3 also saw the object and confirmed
the pilots' description.

On 2 July 1952 at 11.10a.m., Navy Warrant Officer D.C.
Newhouse was out walking with his wife near the Salt Lake some
seven miles from Utah, when they saw a formation of round,
flashing objects in the sky.

Newhouse knew quite a lot about aircraft since he was
stationed at an air supply depot in Oakland, to which he was
attached as a naval photographer. He was quite certain that it
was not a formation of aircraft he was seeing, since the objects
were round and seemed to be flying at supersonic speed.

Newhouse took his sixteen millimetre cine camera, fitted a
telephoto lens, and filmed about forty feet of film of the twelve to
fourteen flying objects. Before he finished, he turned the camera
on one of the objects which peeled off from the formation and
suddenly flew back in the opposite direction. When Newhouse
swung his camera back to the formation again, it had disappeared.

After Newhouse had developed his film he sent it to Project
Blue Book for evaluation. For three months it was subjected to
searching scrutiny by experts, and at the end of this the
possibility of a forgery was considered to be totally excluded.
Also, the Navy's Photo Interpretation Laboratory (P.I.L.)
analysed the film in over a thousand man-hours of work.
Diagrams of each of the 1,600 frames of the film were used to
measure the relative movement of the objects and the variations
in light intensity which they produced. As a result, conventional
objects could be definitively excluded. The P.I.L.'s written
analysis stated unequivocally that the filmed objects had been
'unidentified flying objects under intelligent control'.

Two years earlier, on 15 August 1950, the so-called Montana
film had been taken of two U.F.O.s over Great Falls in Montana. This film was also thoroughly analysed by the P.I.L. and
all possibility of a forgery excluded.

These films are sensational enough in themselves, but the following cases, which disturbed the Blue Book experts, were for Professor Morris K. Jessup unmistakable evidence of the reality of U.F.O.s.

Possibly the most exciting of these was the experience of Panam Captain William B. Nash and his co-pilot, W. Fortenberry on 15 July 1952. On the evening of that day they were ferrying an old DC-4 from New York to Miami.

Visibility was unusually good that evening as the machine approached Newport News, Virginia, at an altitude of 8,000 feet. Nash was pointing out the landmarks to his co-pilot, who was travelling this route for the first time. The two men could see the lights of Norfolk and Newport News in the distance.

The clock on the instrument panel read 21.12 hours as Nash and Fortenberry saw a strange gleam of light ahead of them and directly afterwards made out six apparently glowing metal discs approaching at lightning speed. They were flying on a course about a mile beneath the airliner and compared with objects on the ground 2,000 feet beneath the saucers, seemed to have a diameter of about a hundred feet.

The six U.F.O.s were flying in a V formation when the leading object sighted the airliner. It abruptly reduced speed and the two following saucers wobbled briefly. Both the DC-4 pilots had the impression that they had nearly collided with the leading saucer, having registered too late a signal to slow down. The bright gleam of the objects changed during the 'braking manoeuvre' into a dull glow.

All six of them then banked as if at a single command, altered their course through 150 degrees and disappeared.

Shortly afterwards two more objects appeared under the DC-4 and caught up with the formation in two or three seconds. While doing so they shone more brightly than the others.

Nash and Fortenberry had immediately radioed the control

tower in Norfolk. They then calculated the speed of the U.F.O.s, using a Dalton computer (a circular slide-rule used by air navigators). From the moment of their sighting by the DC-4 pilots to their disappearance, the objects had covered some forty-five miles in fifteen seconds. This made an unbelievable speed of 11,000 m.p.h. which the pilots mentioned only hesitantly in their official reports. To the press, Nash and Fortenberry were considerably more reticent, mentioning only a speed of 'something over 900 m.p.h.'.

To the surprise of the DC-4 pilots, however, the Air Force experts showed no surprise either at the fantastic speed of the U.F.O.s or at their unbelievable manoeuvres.

Nash and Fortenberry were convinced that the objects they had seen could only be intelligently guided spacecraft. And they were both agreed that no man could have physically withstood the lightning manoeuvres they performed.

On 5 August 1962, one of the most breathtaking U.F.O. sightings in the Far East began shortly before midnight over what was then the Haneda Air Force base and is now Tokyo International Airport.

Two flight control officials who were on night duty were running across the tarmac to the control tower when they suddenly noticed a bright light over the Bay of Tokyo. As soon as they saw that it was moving they ran to the control tower where their colleagues were still on duty, in order to observe it more closely through binoculars.

The light seemed to be issuing from a dark, round shape, which slowly approached the airfield and then hovered over it. The watchers could now make out a second smaller light on the underside of the dark shadow. The object moved in an easterly direction and disappeared, then came back for a few seconds, disappeared again and came back for a third time.

The air traffic officials called the radar watch from the tower and learned that they had a U.F.O. on their screen. The object was followed by radar for about five minutes as it flew to and fro over the Bay of Tokyo. Shortly after midnight an F-94 jet fighter was sent up from Johnson Air Force base to observe the object more closely, and managed to track the U.F.O. for about a minute and a half, before it sped away. Shortly afterwards both the air traffic officials and the radar operators sighted the U.F.O. again, before it finally disappeared from view.

In the night of 23 November 1953 an F-89 jet fighter took off from Kinross air base in pursuit of a U.F.O. over the northern part of Lake Michigan. The pilot, Lieutenant Felix Moncla, was accompanied by a radar observer, Lieutenant R. Wilson. Directed by ground radar, Moncla followed the U.F.O. at a speed of 500 m.p.h.

A few minutes later an observer in the G.C.I. (Ground Control Intercept) radar station was surprised to see the two dots representing the jet fighter and the U.F.O. suddenly merge into a single point on his screen. This point finally disappeared from the screen as the U.F.O. moved away at fantastic speed. The radar observer immediately radioed for assistance, assuming that there had been a collision and hoping that the crew of the fighter had baled out in time.

American and Canadian aircraft searched the area from end to end in the hope of finding the crew, or pieces of wreckage or oil slicks. At daybreak boats were sent out on to the lake to join the search. But not the slightest trace of the fighter or its crew was ever found.

At 5 p.m. on 29 June 1954 the B.O.A.C. airliner Centaurus left Idlewild Airport in New York, bound for London. Its captain was James Howard, one of B.O.A.C.'s most experienced pilots. Some of the passengers were already asleep when, shortly after

9 p.m., Captain Howard noticed a group of U.F.O.s – a large object accompanied by a number of smaller ones. He pointed them out to his co-pilot, Lee Boyd, who had in fact already noticed them. The objects were five miles away from the Centaurus and were flying on a parallel course in the same direction. The large object was in the centre with the smaller ones holding station in a circle around it. They continued flying parallel to the Centaurus for about eight miles. The outline of the large object seemed to change from time to time, and Captain Howard thought it probable that it had altered its wing angle and this gave the impression of a change in shape. Simultaneously with this, the smaller objects were seen to change their position.

Howard radioed the air base at Goose Bay in Labrador and asked whether there were any fighters or other aircraft in the vicinity. He learned that this was not the case, but Goose Bay agreed to send up a reconnaissance plane. In the meantime, the other members of the crew – navigation officer George Allen, radio operator Douglas Cox, first engineer Dan Godfrey and second engineer Bill Stewart had all seen the U.F.O.s. The stewardess also caught a glimpse of them and later said that she had never seen anything like it in her two years of flying experience.

Shortly before the reconnaissance plane arrived, the smaller objects withdrew. The navigation officer, who had observed them continuously, told the captain of the Centaurus that they seemed to have disappeared into the interior of the large object. Finally, Howard had to radio the American aircraft to inform the pilot that the large object had disappeared at a fantastic speed.

In addition to eight crew members, fourteen of the passengers on the Centaurus had also observed this amazing incident. The U.F.O.s had followed a parallel course to the airliner for eighteen minutes, over a distance of fifty miles.

Howard said: 'It was a solid thing, I'm sure of that,

manoeuverable and controlled intelligently – a sort of base ship linked somehow with those smaller attendant satellites. There is no rational explanation – except on the basis of spaceships and flying saucers.'

A strange signal appeared on the radar screen at Griffith Air Force base in New York State at midday on 1 July 1954. An F-94 jet was sent up immediately and guided to the object's position by ground control. At the same time the observer of the F-94 followed the object on his own radar. Two minutes after take-off, the pilot saw a gleaming, disc-shaped object high above him. He altered course and climbed towards it. Nothing happened, until the observer radioed to the U.F.O. to identify itself. The object remained motionless, becoming more and more clearly visible as the jet drew nearer. Then suddenly the jet engine cut out and the cockpit started to get hot, although the instruments showed no indication of a fire. The pilot tried to contact base, but nothing happened. He shouted to the radar observer to bale out. Seconds after the latter had ejected, the pilot felt a shock. Gasping for air and with tears in his eyes, he opened the ejector seat and cast a last look at the gigantic round object as he floated to earth. Both airmen landed safely near the town of Walesville in New York State. The F-94 landed on two houses and a car and killed two children and two adults.

At 10 p.m. on 13 August 1956, the air traffic control centre at Lakenheath in England received a message from the ground control station twenty-five miles away that it had a radar trace of an object moving at over 4,000 m.p.h. The object was simultaneously sighted from above by a C-47, and was estimated to be flying at an altitude of 6,500 feet. Finally both stations had the object on their screens. They immediately made contact with a number of other radar units, in order to make comparative checks on the object's progress.

Next a De Havilland Venom night fighter was sent up and

directed towards the U.F.O. by radar. The pilot radioed that he had the object on his inboard radar screen and could also see it directly ahead of him. Then the U.F.O. moved behind the fighter and sat firmly on its tail, following its every manoeuvre. The ground stations had the U.F.O. and the night fighter on their screens simultaneously for ten minutes, until the pilot ran out of fuel and had to land.

A second night fighter was sent up to replace the Venom, but had to land again with engine trouble. Finally the U.F.O. took a northerly course and disappeared from the radar screen.

The ground staff had simultaneously followed the object with the naked eye and described it as a round, brightly shining disc. The radar observers identified it as a concrete object on their screens and tracked it as it moved. The pilot of the night fighter also saw it on the radar screen of his machine, and with his own eyes.

'The Lakenheath case involved two independent ground-radar operators, one military pilot and one air control tower operator,' says Professor Allen J. Hynek, scientific adviser to Project Blue Book. 'This is the most puzzling and unusual case in the radar-visual files. The apparently rational, intelligent behaviour of the U.F.O. suggests a mechanical device of unknown origin as the most probable explanation of this sighting.'

At 7.21 p.m. on 4 September 1957, four jet fighters took off from the Ota military base in Portugal on a night navigation flight. This was a routine practice flight which was to take the aircraft as far as Granada in Spain and back over the Portuguese towns of Portalegre and Coruche at an altitude of 26,000 feet. Captain Jose Lemos Ferreira led the operation, in which three other pilots took part. The night was clear and starlit. The first leg of the flight went smoothly according to plan, and over Granada the planes turned and made for Portalegre. It was here that

Captain Ferreira noticed an unusually large light on the horizon
to his left. He observed it for a few minutes and then radioed the
other machines to call it to their attention. The left wing pilot
had already seen it.

The centre of the strange object changed colour constantly
from dark green to blue, yellow and red. Suddenly it became
larger, growing five or six times its original size. Then, before the
pilots realized what was happening it shrank to a small, scarcely
visible yellow point. This process was repeated a couple of times,
during which the object's position with relation to the jet
fighters did not change. The U.F.O.'s position was forty degrees
to port of the aircraft. Captain Ferreira was unable to make out
whether the changes in size were taking place on the spot or were
due to the object's movement. After changing size constantly for
six or seven minutes, the object disappeared over the horizon at
about ninety degrees to port of the fighters.

At 10.38 p.m., shortly before Portalegre, the captain decided
to change course for Coruche. The jets made a fifty-degree turn
to port, only to find the U.F.O. still in its position at ninety
degrees to their course. Captain Ferreira was now convinced
that it could not be a stationary object. It was giving off a bright
red light and was well beneath the altitude of the fighters.

When the pilots had been on their new course for a few
minutes, a smaller U.F.O. suddenly detached itself from the
large one, and before they had recovered from their astonishment, three more similar objects appeared on the big U.F.O.'s
right side. The whole formation changed speed constantly as it
moved.

As the fighters were approaching Coruche, the big U.F.O.
suddenly dived away at high speed, then immediately rose again
just as fast towards the fighters.

The pilots were thrown into confusion, and almost broke
formation in their attempts to sideslip away from the U.F.O.
But as soon as they crossed its path, the U.F.O. withdrew
together with its satellites.

The whole performance had lasted some forty minutes, and all the pilots were agreed that there could be no rational explanation for it. Captain Ferreira rejected all the customary explanations – the planet Venus, a balloon, unfamiliar aircraft etc. – which are so often given after U.F.O. sightings.

All these incidents were naturally kept secret by the U.S. Air Force, and it was only years later – after Project Blue Book had been disbanded – that they were finally made public.

As early as 1953, the C.I.A. decided that drastic action must be taken to prevent the truth about U.F.O.s from becoming known.

And a contributing factor in this decision was undoubtedly an unusual incident involving the Secretary for the Navy, Dan Kimball.

It happened in April 1952, when Kimball was flying with his entire staff to Hawaii. Rear Admiral Arthur Radford was following in a second aircraft. Suddenly two disc-shaped U.F.O.s appeared, flew several times round Kimball's machine and sped away towards the second Navy plane which was following fifty miles behind. There they performed the same manoeuvre, circling the machine carrying Radford several times before disappearing 'unbelievably fast' as the Navy pilots said. They estimated the U.F.O.s' speed at about 1,800 m.p.h.

As soon as Kimball had landed in Hawaii, he radioed a report of the incident to the Air Force, which was already officially engaged in the investigation of the U.F.O. phenomenon. Back in Washington, he enquired through one of his adjutants what action was being taken, and in answer he was given to understand by the Air Force and the C.I.A. that it would be better for him not to have seen anything if he wanted to stay in office.

Kimball promptly arranged an interview with Admiral Calvin Bolster, chief of the Office of Naval Research (O.N.R.), and the latter now ordered a thorough investigation of all

U.F.O. sightings within the Navy's sphere of influence. The inquiries instituted as a result of Bolster's order came to the conclusion that U.F.O.s were a real phenomenon and were indeed unidentified, intelligently controlled flying objects.

The Navy delivered its evaluation of the situation with this conclusion to the Air Force in the autumn of 1952, and the Air Force immediately requested the Navy not to undertake any further steps until it had completed its own researches through Project Blue Book. Commenting on the C.I.A.'s subsequent activities, retired U.S. Marine Corps Major Donald E. Keyhoe, the long-standing director of the N.I.C.A.P. (National Investigations Committee on Aerial Phenomena) said:

Even though the Kimball threat seemed ended, the C.I.A. knew another Navy fight could erupt, and the A.F. had shown it was not tough enough to cope with such a danger. The only answer was to seize control of the A.F. investigation and insist on a hard-boiled, ruthless censorship, to kill off public belief in U.F.O.s.

To carry this out, the C.I.A. arranged a meeting of scientists and A.F. representatives at the Pentagon, for a confidential analysis of the U.F.O. evidence ... The C.I.A.-selected scientists were known sceptics. Most of them had no real knowledge of U.F.O.s and they considered the subject nonsense. Since the C.I.A. agents would have full authority, they could limit and offset the evidence, steering the scientists towards a completely negative verdict. The agency heads had little doubt of the outcome.

This C.I.A.-controlled committee sat from 14 to 18 January 1953 and was named the Robertson Panel, after its Chairman, Professor H.P. Robertson, a physicist at the California Institute of Technology who was also employed as a weapons system specialist by the C.I.A. Other members of the panel included C.I.A. agent P.G. Strong, A.T.I.C. intelligence chief General

Garland, C.I.A. employees Dr H. Marshall Chadwell and Ralph L. Clark, the physicist Professor Samuel A. Goudsmit and the Professor of Astronomy at Chicago University, Thornton Page. Ruppelt, Fournet and Hynek were also present.

In the closing report of the Robertson Panel, the C.I.A. insisted on denying the existence of U.F.O.s on the grounds that widespread reports of sightings were 'hindering news channels and endangering national security'. Also, the fear was voiced that Russia could manipulate such a situation in case of war. The report also urged the institution of a programme of playing down and ridiculing the U.F.O. programme in order to reduce public interest. In order to remove the halo of mystery surrounding the sightings, mass media such as radio, television, film and newspapers were to be brought into play.

Major Dewey Fournet later said: 'We were double-crossed. The C.I.A. doesn't want to prepare the public – they're trying to bury the subject. Those agents ran the whole show and the scientists followed their lead . . . I know those C.I.A. agents were only following orders, but once or twice I almost blew up.'

Commenting on the real intentions of the C.I.A. and the Air Force, Keyhoe said: 'When the A.F. realized that U.F.O.s were spacecraft, in the early years, the Air Defense Command was determined to capture one of these superior machines. This was confirmed to me in a personal conference with General Sory Smith, Deputy Director of Information, and Major Jeremiah Boggs, a headquarters intelligence officer. In contrast with the later denials, Boggs frankly admitted that the A.F. had put out a special order for its pilots to capture U.F.O.s: "We were naturally anxious to get hold of one of the things. We told pilots to do practically anything in reason, even if they had to grab one by the tail."'

Is Keyhoe to be believed? The U.S. Air Force itself seemed convinced that he was, as witness the following statement:

We in the Air Force recognise Major Keyhoe as a responsible, accurate reporter. His long association and cooperation with the Air Force, in our study of unidentified flying objects, qualifies him as a leading civilian authority on this investigation.

All the sighting reports and other information he has listed have been cleared and made available to Major Keyhoe from Air Technical Intelligence records, at his request.

The Air Force, and its investigating agency, Project Blue Book, is aware of Major Keyhoe's conclusion that the 'flying saucers' are from another planet. The Air Force has never denied that this possibility exists. Some of the personnel believe that there may be some strange natural phenomena completely unknown to us, but that if the apparently controlled manoeuvres reported by competent observers are correct, then the only remaining explanation is the interplanetary answer.

Signed Albert M. Chop
Air Force Press Office

8

The Net

Different nations, in particular the Russians, Americans, Canadians, English, French and Dutch, tried to uncover the technological secret of the U.F.O.s. The U.S. Air Force made intensive efforts to capture a U.F.O. with this object, but probably the most determined of all nations was the Soviet Union. After their interceptors had consistently failed to force one down, both the Russians and Americans resorted to more drastic methods and gave the order to open fire on U.F.O.s in the hope of bringing one down with its propulsion unit still intact. In 1957 Senator Lee Metcalf asked the Air Force whether its pilots were still pursuing U.F.O.s, and received a written reply from Major General Joe W. Kelly which stated: 'Air Force interceptors still pursue unidentified flying objects as a matter of security to this country and to determine the technical aspects involved.'

Major Keyhoe was informed of the following incident by a private source in the Air Force:

We too have fired on U.F.O.s. About 10 o'clock one morning a radar site near a fighter base picked up a U.F.O. doing 700 m.p.h. The U.F.O. then slowed to 100 m.p.h. and two

F-80s were scrambled to intercept. Eventually one F-80 closed on the U.F.O. at about 3,000 feet altitude. The U.F.O. began to accelerate away but the pilot still managed to get within 500 yards of the object for a short period of time. It was definitely saucer-shaped. As the pilot pushed the F-80 at top speed the U.F.O. began to pull away. When the range reached 1,000 yards the pilot armed his guns and fired in an attempt to down the saucer. He failed, and the U.F.O. pulled away rapidly, vanishing in the distance.

The Soviet High Command also hoped to force a U.F.O. to land without completely destroying it. On 24 July 1957, for instance, anti-aircraft batteries in the Kuril Islands opened fire on a U.F.O. formation, but the shining objects moved away rapidly without sustaining any damage.

The Royal Canadian Air Force even went so far as to build a landing place for U.F.O.s near Suffield, Alberta, in collaboration with the Defence Research Board. The Canadians hoped to lure U.F.O.s to the ground by means of special signals. This secret project went under the name of Project Second Storey.

A spokesman for the R.A.F. declared that their five-year programme of U.F.O. research was now completed, but the results were being withheld from the public to avoid creating any more controversy on the subject. Besides which, they could not be sufficiently explained without giving away top secret information.

But Air Chief Marshal Lord Dowding was less reticent: 'The existence of these machines is proved, and I have accepted it absolutely,' he said.

Similarly, on 16 January 1957, the American Admiral Delmer Fahrney stated: 'Reliable reports indicate that they are objects which penetrate our atmosphere at very high speeds and are controlled by thinking, intelligent beings.'

The press officer for Project Blue Book himself admitted:

'One thing is absolutely sure: we are being observed by beings from outer space.'

And Captain Ruppelt, the former director of Blue Book, who was inevitably forced to toe the official line, later asked:

> What constitutes proof? Does a U.F.O. have to land at the River Entrance to the Pentagon, near the Joint Chiefs of Staff offices? Or is it proof when a ground radar station detects a U.F.O., sends a jet to intercept it, the jet pilot sees it, and locks on with his radar, only to have the U.F.O. streak away at phenomenal speed? Is it proof when a jet pilot fires at a U.F.O. and sticks to his story even under the threat of court-martial. Does this constitute proof?

Jessup was becoming more and more isolated. He knew that extraterrestrial spaceships were watching the earth and had appeared repeatedly in every historical age. He also knew through his connections that the military was in possession of the same knowledge. However, neither the public nor his colleagues were aware of this. In fact he had even been accused of becoming obsessed with U.F.O.s, and allowing his preoccupation with them to interfere with his work. He was labelled as an outsider. Jessup ignored the critics – he knew that they were not in possession of the same background information as he was. And he felt it his duty to inform the public.

Jessup wrote a book, *The Case for the U.F.O.*, which was published by the Citadel Press in New York in 1955, and which marked the beginning of the mysterious affair in which Jessup became more and more embroiled. After the book appeared, Jessup received a series of handwritten letters which were sent by a certain Carl M. Allen, but signed with the name of Carlos Miguel Allende. These letters mostly dealt with the origin of U.F.O.s, but also made reference to one or two incidents during the Second World War which were known to Jessup; perhaps it was for this reason that he took these letters more seriously than he would otherwise have done. Allen or Allende alluded in particular to an experiment carried out by the Navy in October 1943 in the naval harbour at Philadelphia.

During the Second World War, the Office of Naval Research (O.N.R.) urgently requested proposals from independent scientists which could be used in developing camouflage methods for warships.

An unnamed scientist supposedly visited O.N.R. officials at this time in order to demonstrate 'the perfect camouflage'. As he was one of the most distinguished scientific researchers in the U.S.A., his proposals were taken seriously and tried out in a series of experiments. The scientist supposedly made reference to 'effects of the Einsteinian unified field theory, according to which it is possible to use an electromagnetic field, not only to make objects invisible, but also to effect alterations in space and time'. The U.S. destroyer *Eldridge* was supposedly moved several times from Philadelphia to Norfolk and back by this method. Allende wrote to Jessup:

During the experiment in October 1943, the U.S. destroyer *Eldridge*, together with its crew, was made to disappear from the naval harbour in Philadelphia, by a magnetic field in the form of a rotational ellipsoid. A magnetic field of ninety metres radius enclosed the ship. Within this sphere, everyone on board saw each other fleetingly disappear into a bottomless nothingness. Outside, directly on the edge of this force field, I could make out nothing except the shape of the ship's hull clearly delineated in the water.

According to Allende, it had been possible to alter the molecular structure of matter so that the *Eldridge* disappeared together with every soul on board. Allende's letter stated that the men on the *Eldridge* had undergone a fearful fate. Many of them had turned into flaming torches or lost their reason and jumped overboard. The few survivors had ended up in mental hospitals. The experiment had been a total failure for the Navy, as it had put the ship completely out of commission.

Jessup's publication of the Allende letters galvanized the Pentagon into activity. Admiral Ranson Bennett, chief of the O.N.R., received the book from an officer, together with marginal notes by three different people referring to the Allende letters. When Bennett asked what it was all about, he was told that they related to the 'Philadelphia Experiment'.

He immediately rang a secret number and only two hours later Pentagon officials, military staff, leading scientists and personnel from the F.B.I. and C.I.A. gathered for a top-level secret conference.

On the same day F.B.I. agents flew to New Kensington in Pennsylvania, from where the Allende letters had been sent, in an effort to trace Allen alias Allende. Some of the local inhabitants remembered the little man with the Southern appearance who had lodged with an elderly couple named Carter. The Carters had lived on a farm on the edge of the village for forty years, but when the F.B.I. agents reached the farm, both they and Allende had disappeared. Enquiries among the local police revealed that the Carters had been considered an amiable couple, but seldom or never came into the village to shop, never once made contact with their immediate neighbours, and had not made a single friend in the forty years they had been there. When asked what they looked like, the neighbours could only describe them as 'an elderly married couple with a dark complexion', exactly like Allende. They were generally considered to be 'strange people', but no one could say exactly why.

The F.B.I. agents finally gave up the search for Allende; they had not been told the reason for seeking him. Apart from F.B.I. chief J. Edgar Hoover and two of his closest colleagues, no one had been informed of the background to the affair.

In 1957, Jessup was called to Washington once more by the

Office of Naval Research and asked whether he had been responsible for the marginal notes in the copy of his book which had been sent to Admiral Bennett.

Jessup stated that he knew nothing about them, and once again assured the O.N.R. that he had never spoken personally to Allende. But this the Navy already knew.

Such was the basis of this mysterious affair, an experiment which never took place, but which is repeatedly being brought out as hard evidence.

After careful research, I have come to the conclusion that the whole thing was a deliberate piece of mystification, a refined way of discrediting Jessup engineered by the Secret Service as a result of the decisions of the Robertson Panel. At that time it was simply unthinkable that a distinguished scientist should be in a position to publish classified information about the U.F.O. phenomenon. Jessup represented a serious danger, and so Allende was 'invented' to lure Jessup into a trap, baited with a convincing foundation of scientific fact.

As expected, Jessup became more and more embroiled in his investigations of the Philadelphia Experiment, and made a thorough fool of himself.

The mysterious Allende now lives in Mexico, and has admitted that the whole affair was a fabrication by the Secret Service. The extent of the intelligence services' interest in the U.F.O. field is demonstrated by the experience of N.I.C.A.P. adviser Ralph Mayher, which was not an isolated instance. C.I.A. agents were constantly on the look-out for U.F.O. material which was either suppressed or made use of as demanded by the U.F.O. policy of the time. In 1957 C.I.A. agents asked Mayher to give them a U.F.O. film which was due to be technically analysed by the Air Force. Mayher was promised that the film would be returned to him by the Air Force, together with the technical analysis. But apart from a portion of the film from which the best shots had been cut, Mayher received nothing.

C.I.A. agents were also active at the N.I.C.A.P. office in Washington, where they would appear at irregular intervals on the look-out for confidential material.

Naturally there were sceptics then as there are today – people who dismissed any suggestion of an official cover-up as U.F.O. fanatics' persecution mania. The same sceptics rightly ask why U.F.O.s – if they are really extraterrestrial spaceships – do not land in order to make contact with us.

This brings me to the strangest and least believable aspect of the whole U.F.O. phenomenon. The scientific integrity of this book would hardly suffer if I made no reference at all to 'close encounters of the third kind' – reports of actual contact with extraterrestrial life forms.

Unfortunately one cannot simply omit facts just because one does not agree with them or because they do not fit in with one's preconceived ideas. Can one disbelieve reports of meetings with the occupants of U.F.O.s, yet be willing to accept reports of other meetings with U.F.O.s?

Plain common sense, of course, leads to rejection of the thought of humanoid beings – mockingly referred to as little green men. They tend to discredit the whole U.F.O. concept. U.F.O.s may really exist, people say, but surely not humanoids. But if the occupants of U.F.O.s are merely figments of imagination, then so must be more commonplace U.F.O. sightings. But there are so many reliable witnesses for these that they cannot be regarded as mere inventions.

In the words of J. Allen Hynek in *The U.F.O. Experience*: 'Are these people all affected by some strange "virus" that does not attack "sensible" people? What a strange sickness this must be, attacking people in all walks of life, regardless of training or vocation.'

There are really two main groups of so-called 'contactees'. The first are men who never had any interest in the U.F.O. phenomenon and only became involved in it by chance. Mostly they are merely surprised by their 'close encounter' and are reluctant to admit its reality. Generally they draw no conclusions from it, and do not try to make capital out of it through the press or in any other way. After their encounter, which often becomes public only by chance, they sink back into the anonymity from which they had briefly emerged.

Close examination of these experiences seldom reveals contradictions or falsifications. The statements made by these contactees cannot usually be faulted by the use of investigatory methods such as hypnosis, lie detectors or truth drugs, but their authenticity still cannot be proved beyond doubt.

In any case, encounters of this type frequently involve a number of people.

For people in the second group, U.F.O.s have become part of their lives. For them, a close encounter is an act of illumination, after which they behave like a prophet returned from the wilderness to proclaim universal salvation. They are only too ready to describe their (imagined) journey through space with 'Blue-eyed Rheda' or 'Arkon with the long blond hair' and the mysterious 'Messengers of the Omnipresent Brothers'. Surrounded by a host of fellow believers, they act as high priest of their U.F.O. club, give lectures, write books about their experiences, found U.F.O. sects, allow themselves to be fêted at U.F.O. congresses, court the press and generally cash in on their experiences. They produce 'U.F.O.' pictures made by photographing a dustbin lid thrown in the air, and blurred rear views of people from Venus or planet X.

One might expect these U.F.O. converts to show a degree of solidarity but in fact they are all deadly enemies. One man's version of salvation is seldom another's, and the exponents of the good tidings from outer space are every bit as sectarian as the sidewalk evangelists with their half-digested truths.

The excesses to which these 'extraterrestrial tidings' can lead is demonstrated by the following curious occurrence, which took place in the summer of 1944, when half Europe lay in ruins.

Every morning in the secluded gardens of a villa near London, six nubile girls lay down naked on couches in the rays of the early morning sun. There they remained throughout the day, their legs receptively spread, reading the Bible. As soon as the sun had gone down, they dressed silently and left the garden. Their places were taken by other naked figures, who again with Bible in hand exposed themselves to the moonlight.

The villa's owner, Lady R., was convinced that these young, virgin figures would be impregnated by the seed of cosmic beings who had descended to earth on sunbeams or moonbeams. Unfortunately her hopes of conceiving a heavenly being remained unfulfilled.

Other U.F.O. sectarians in this group include those who 'have set their watches by space time', whatever that may mean. They reckon time in light-years, apparently exist outside the confines of time and space, and are also acquainted with the love-life of the Venusians, from personal experience, of course.

Although these 'contactees' tend to bring the whole U.F.O. field into ridicule, we should not perhaps be too hard on them. They are basically harmless, and it requires no great psychological insight to discover their motives. They are driven by loneliness, complexes, desire for attention, the hope of a saviour – all the customary bases of an ersatz religion. We should treat them with understanding and tolerance, for it is our own society with its increasing alienation which is largely responsible for their behaviour.

Naturally it is the contactees in the first group who are the most interesting. Significantly, most of their descriptions of the inhabitants of U.F.O.s contain the same distinguishing features. Whatever part of the world they come from, they usually refer to small, humanoid beings dressed in shining, overall-like garments, and mostly carrying transparent helmets. In almost all instances, the place of the sighting is familiar to the eyewitnesses. They are frequently at work when they become aware of the U.F.O. The number of contact reports is equally divided between persons of both sexes, and there have frequently been close encounters with children.

Allen Hynek has even found similarities of behaviour by the U.F.O. crews in the different reports:

The reader ... will find the occupants reportedly picking up samples of earth and rocks and carrying them aboard their craft, much as U.S. astronauts picked up moon rocks; he will find them seemingly exhibiting interest in human installations and vehicles; he will even find them making off with rabbits, dogs, and fertilizer!

It would be helpful, if we could demonstrate that close encounters of the third kind differ systematically from the other five U.F.O. categories ... But they do not differ in any way – by geographical distribution, by times of occurrence, in numbers, and especially in *kinds* of observers.

Hynek has divided 'close encounters' into the following categories:

Close encounters of the first kind:
    a U.F.O. sighting at a great distance.
Close encounters of the second kind:
    observation of a U.F.O. at close quarters.
Close encounters of the third kind:
    cases in which contact with U.F.O. crew members takes
    place inside or outside the object.

The fact that close encounters of the third kind usually seem to involve humanoid beings is perhaps the hardest for us to swallow. Even if we are prepared to admit that U.F.O. crews are of extraterrestrial origin, surely it is too much to expect that they will look like human beings. Would it not be too much of a coincidence for intelligent beings which have developed in a world light-years away (for the earth is undoubtedly the only populated planet in our solar system) to have similar physiological characteristics: arms, legs, eyes, nose, mouth, and even similar sexual characteristics?

There are, however, several prominent scientists according to whom we should accept this similarity between intelligent beings from different worlds as fact. Professor Roland Puccetti, a contributor to the famous journals, *The Philosophical Quarterly* and *Analysis,* argues in his book, *Persons,* that on the basis of the principles of convergence in evolution a great similarity must be assumed between us and extraterrestrial beings. They will – just like us – be the descendants of land-bound predators and therefore also have a tendency to attack others bodily when they are in danger of being injured themselves. As they will be a biological species, which while differing from *Homo sapiens* is nevertheless very similar to him, there is no reasonable ground to assume that such extraterrestrial societies would not be characterized by extensive similarities of their individual members in relation to bodily strength and intelligence, even though there could naturally be considerable differences between the individual societies.

Puccetti bases his arguments on the thesis that similar external conditions lead to the development of similar forms and organs in genetically different life forms. This principle of convergence would mean that on all Earth-like planets in the Universe, life forms would emerge which, as a result of their struggle for survival, would develop similar characteristics to those on Earth: plants with a stem and leaves, and 'animals' with limbs and heads. Higher life forms would in the course of time develop sense organs and intelligence, in order to deal with their problems.

The Nobel prize-winner and biochemist, Joshua Lederberg, the biochemist Dr Joseph Kraut of California University, and the well known biologist Dr Robert Bieri have all come to similar conclusions.

Thus the idea of extraterrestrial humanoids is not so outlandish as it may seem. But even so, reports of close encounters with extraterrestrials leave us uneasy and at a loss for words.

9

The Fantastic Encounter of Antônio Villas Boas

In Rio de Janeiro, on the afternoon of 22 February 1958, Antônio Villas Boas made the following statement in the surgery of one Dr Fontes, witnessed by the doctor himself and the journalist João Martins.

My name is Antônio Villas Boas, I am twenty-three years old and a farmer by profession. I live with my family on a farm which belongs to us. It is situated near the town of São Francisco de Sales in the state of Minas Gerais, near the border of the state of São Paulo. I have two brothers and three sisters, who all live in the neighbourhood; another brother and sister are dead. All the male members of the family work on the farm. There are many fields and plantations belonging to it which must be cultivated. We have a petrol-driven tractor, which we use in two shifts when the fields have to be tilled. The farm workers we employ work during the day. At night I plough mostly alone or with one of my brothers. I am unmarried and in good health, work hard, am taking a correspondence course and study as often as I can. It was a sacrifice for me to come to Rio, as I am urgently needed on the farm. But I thought it my duty to report on the unusual events in which I was involved. I will do everything which you, senhores, think right – and I am also ready to make a declaration to the civil or military authorities.

It all began on the night of 5 October 1957. On that evening we had visitors and for this reason did not go to bed until 11 o'clock – much later than usual. I was in my room together with my brother João. As it was very hot, I opened the shutters of the windows giving on to the farmyard. There, in the middle of the yard, I saw a blinding light, which lit up the whole area. It was much brighter than moonlight, and I could not work out where it came from. It must have come from somewhere above, and had the effect of searchlights directed downwards and lighting up everything beneath them. But there was nothing to be seen in the sky. I called my brother and told him about it, but nothing would make him stir from his rest and he merely said it would be better to go to sleep. So I closed the shutters and we both lay down to sleep. But I was unable to rest, and plagued by curiosity I stood up after a while and opened the shutters again. The light was still in the same place and had not changed. I continued to stare out at it and suddenly it moved on to my window. I hastily closed the shutters in alarm, and made so much noise in doing so that my brother, who had already gone to sleep, woke up again. We both watched in the darkened room as the light streamed through the slits in the shutters, then moved up towards the roof and finally gleamed through the tiles. [Brazilian farmhouses are open from the ground to the roof and, because of the hot climate and for better ventilation, have no false ceilings.] Finally the light disappeared and did not return.

On 14 October the second occurrence took place. It must have been between 9.30 and 10.00 p.m. I do not know exactly as I had no watch. I was working with another of my brothers in the field with the tractor. Suddenly we saw a very bright light, which shone so much that our eyes hurt. When we first became aware of it, it was large and round – like a wagon wheel – standing at the northern end of the field. It was bright red and lit up a large area. Something could be made out in the light, but I cannot say for certain whether this was so, since I was far too blinded by it. I asked my brother to go over with me and have a look. But he didn't want to. So I went alone. When I came nearer to the thing, it suddenly moved and changed to the southern end of the field at enormous speed, where it stood still again. I ran after it and the same manoeuvre was repeated. This time it moved back to its original position. I tried again, but the same thing happened twenty times. Eventually I got tired of it and went back to my brother. The light remained stationary in the distance for a few minutes. From time to time it seemed to send out rays in all directions, like the rays of the setting sun. Then it suddenly disappeared as if it had been switched off. But I am not quite sure whether it all really happened like that, since I am no longer sure whether I kept looking in that direction without a break. Perhaps I might have looked away for a short time, and it could then have quickly risen up and have disappeared when I looked again.

On the next day, 15 October, I was ploughing alone with the tractor in the same field. It was a cold night and the sky was clear and starlit. At exactly 1 o'clock, I suddenly saw a red star, which looked exactly like one of those big bright stars. But I quickly noticed that it was no star, since it got larger and larger, apparently coming nearer. In a few moments it became a shining, egg-shaped object, which was flying towards me at a fantastic speed. It approached so quickly that it was over the tractor before I could think what to do. Suddenly the object stopped and sank down to about fifty metres or so above my head. The tractor and the field were as brightly lit as if it were midday. The headlight on my tractor was completely swallowed up by the bright red glow. I was very afraid, as I had no idea what it could be. I wanted to drive off with the tractor and escape, but in comparison with the thing over my head it was far too slow. There was no point. If I had jumped down from the tractor and tried to run away across the freshly ploughed field, I would probably have broken a leg.

I sat there uncertainly for some two minutes, wondering what to do, and during this time the object moved again and stopped about ten to fifteen metres in front of the tractor. Then it sank slowly to the ground. It came nearer and nearer, until I could see that it was an unusual, almost round machine with small red lights all the way round.

Directly in front of me was a gigantic red searchlight, which had blinded me when the thing came down from above. It resembled an elongated egg with three spikes at the front – one in the middle and one on either side. These were made of metal and tapered to a point from a broad base. I could not make out their colour, as they were bathed in red light. On top there was something turning very quickly which also emitted reddish fluorescent light.

As the machine slowed down to land, the rotating part also turned more slowly and at the same time I had the impression that the light turned to a greenish colour. At this moment the rotating part looked like a plate or a shallow dome. I do not know whether it really looked like this or whether this impression was merely created by the movement, since the rotating part did not stop moving for a second, even when the flying object had landed.

I naturally did not observe most of the details until later, since at first I was far too excited. I lost the last shreds of my self-control when three metal supports – like a tripod – appeared out of the underside of the object a few metres above the ground. They were metal legs which were obviously meant to bear the weight of the machine on landing. The tractor had been standing with its engine running all this time. I pressed the accelerator, steered it round one side of the flying object and tried to escape. But after a few metres the motor cut out and my headlights were extinguished. I do not know why, since the ignition key was in place and the headlights were switched on. I pressed the starter, but the engine did not fire. I immediately jumped down from the tractor on the side away from the object and ran away. But it was already too late, for I had only taken a few steps when someone grasped me by the arm – a small, strangely dressed being who reached up to my shoulder. I turned in desperation and gave him a push, which made him overbalance. The stranger let go and fell backwards on to the ground. I tried to run away but was grasped by three other strangers simultaneously from behind and from the sides. They held my arms and legs fast and raised me up, and I was unable to defend myself. I twisted and kicked, but they held on tight and did not let go. Then I shouted for help and cursed them, telling them to let me go. My shouting must have surprised them or made them curious, since on the way to the machine they stopped every time I opened my mouth and stared into my face. But they did not release their grip one little bit. At least this gave me some idea of their attitude towards me, and I was somewhat relieved. They dragged me to their machine, which stood some ten metres above the ground on the metal legs I have already described. At the back end of the machine was a door which opened downwards to form a kind of ramp. At the end of it was a metal ladder. It was of the same silvery material as the sides of the machine, and reached to the ground. The aliens had some difficulty in pushing me up it as there was only room for two people to stand on it side by side. Also the ladder was not stiff, but flexible, and swayed violently from side to side as a result of my efforts to tear myself free. On either side was a rail the thickness of a broomstick, and I clung to it, trying to prevent myself from being dragged further up it. This meant that they had to keep stopping in order to prise my hands loose from the rail. This was also flexible, and later, as I came down to the ground again, I had the impression that it was made of pieces inserted into one another.

Finally they made it, and brought me into a small square

room. The gleaming light from the metal ceiling was reflected in the polished metal walls and came from numerous square lamps, which were fixed all around beneath the ceiling.

I was put on the floor. The ladder attached to the entrance door was drawn in and fixed and the door itself raised to close it. The room had daylight lighting, but even in this blinding light one could not see the outline of the door, which after it had been closed melted completely into the wall. I only knew from the metal ladder where it must be.

One of the five people present pointed to an open door and gave me to understand that I should follow them into the next room. I obeyed, for I had no other choice.

So we all went into this room, which was larger than the other and a half oval in shape. The walls here gleamed in the same way. I believe that it was the centre of the machine, for in the middle stood a round, apparently solid pillar which narrowed in the middle. One can hardly suppose that it was only there for decoration. In my opinion it supported the ceiling. The only furniture in the room was an unusually shaped table and several swivelling stools, like one sees in bars. Everything was made from the same metal. The table and stools only had one central pedestal, which in the case of the table was firmly fixed to the floor, while in the case of the stools it was joined to a movable ring by three protruding struts and let into the floor. In this way anyone who sat on them could turn in any direction.

They were still holding on to me tightly and were obviously talking about me. When I say 'talking', what I heard had not the slightest similarity to human speech. Nor can I imitate the way they spoke. Suddenly they seemed to have come to a decision about me. All five of them began to undress me. I tried to stop them, and shouted and cursed. They stopped and looked at me, obviously wishing to make me understand that they are polite people. But that did not prevent them from stripping me to the skin. In doing so they did not hurt me or tear my garments.

Finally I stood there naked, frightened to death, as I did not know what they intended to do with me next. One of them came up to me with something in his hand. It must have been some kind of wet sponge, for he used it to rub a fluid all over my body. It was a very wet sponge, not one of the usual rubber sponges. The fluid was quite clear and odourless, but thicker than water. At first I thought it must be a kind of oil, but that could not have been so as it did not make the skin oily or greasy. When they had rubbed my skin with it, I was freezing cold, for it was a cold night outside and the two rooms in the machine were much colder, still. It would have been bad enough being naked, but the fluid made it even worse. My whole body was trembling, I was so cold. The fluid soon dried, and soon I did not notice it any more.

Three of these people now led me to a door opposite the one by which I had entered the machine. One of them touched something in the middle of the door, which immediately opened on both sides like the flaps of a bar door which when shut reached from the floor to the ceiling. Above it was a kind of inscription of red illuminated signs. The lighting gave the effect of the signs being raised one or two centimetres above the surface of the door. They did not have the slightest similarity to any writing which I know. I tried to remember them, but have forgotten them since.

At any rate I now went with two of these men into a small, square room, which was lit in the same way as the others. As soon as we were there, the doors closed behind us. When I looked round there was no trace of a door to be seen, only a wall which was in no way different to the others.

Suddenly this wall opened again, and through the door came two more men. They were carrying two fairly thick red rubber tubes, each of which was more than a metre long. One of these tubes was connected at one end to a beaker-shaped glass container. At the other end was a mouthpiece which looked like a cupping glass. This was pressed onto my skin at the chin, where you can still see a dark place which is the mark of a scar. Before the man did this he pressed the tube together with his hand as if he wanted to squeeze the air out of it. At first I felt neither a pain nor a prick – I only noticed that my skin was ·sucked in. Later the place began to burn and itch. Finally I discovered that the skin had been injured and scratched. After the rubber tube had been fixed onto me, I watched as the beaker filled half-way up with my blood.

Then they stopped, took this tube off and replaced it by another one. Then more blood was taken from the other side of my chin. You can see the same dark place there as on the other side, senhores. This time the beaker was filled right up. Then the receptacle was removed. The skin was pierced at this spot too, and it burned and itched. Then the men went out. The door closed behind them, and I was alone.

For some time no one paid any attention to me, for more than half an hour at any rate. There was nothing in the room but a large couch – a kind of bed, but without a headboard or frame. As the mattress was arched in the middle, it was not particularly comfortable, but at least it was soft, like foam rubber, and covered with a thick grey material which was also soft.

As I was tired after the struggle and all the excitement, I lay down. At that moment I noticed a strange smell, which made me feel worse. I had the feeling that I was inhaling thick, pungent smoke which threatened to choke me. Perhaps this was really the case, for when I examined the wall, I noticed a number of small metal tubes closed at the end, which projected from the wall on a level with my head and were perforated with many small holes, as in a shower. Grey smoke poured from these holes and dispersed in the air. This was where the smell came from. I did not feel at all well, and became so ill that I had to vomit. I rushed to a corner of the room and threw up. After that I could once again breathe without difficulty. But the smell of the smoke still made me feel ill.

I was very depressed. What could there be in store for me?

Up to that point I still did not have the slightest idea what these strange men actually looked like. All five of them wore very close-fitting overalls made of thick grey stuff, which were very soft and striped with black in various places. They wore helmets of the same colour which came down to their necks. It was made of stiffer material – I do not know what – and was reinforced at the back with thin metal strips. This helmet covered everything except the eyes, which could be seen through two round, spectacle-like lenses. The men stared at me through these lenses with their clear, apparently blue eyes. Above the eyes, the helmet was twice as high as a normal head. There was probably something above the head inside the helmet, which was not visible from the outside. Three round, silver tubes made of metal or rubber, I don't know which, ran from the middle of the head down the back and disappeared into the suit at rib height. The middle tube ran down the spine, the other two to right and left about ten centimetres beneath the armpits. I could not see any bulge or projection which suggested that they could be connected with a container or an instrument concealed beneath the suit.

The sleeves of the overalls were long and narrow. At the wrists they turned into thick five-fingered gloves of the same colour, which undoubtedly hindered the movement of the hands. I noticed for instance that the men could scarcely touch the palms of their hands with the tips of their fingers. But this did not prevent them from grasping me firmly and skilfully or handling the rubber tubes when they drew blood from me.

The overalls must have been a kind of uniform, since all the crew members wore a shield the size of a slice of pineapple. From there a silver-coloured stripe of material or metal foil led to a narrow belt without a buckle. None of the overall-like 'uniforms' had pockets or buttons. The legs were skin-tight and shaped into a kind of tennis shoe at the end without any perceptible join. However, unlike those which we have, they had soles four to seven centimetres thick. The shoes turned upwards slightly at the tips, but not like the buckle shoes in history books. The aliens were able to run around nimbly and without hindrance in them. Only the completely closed overall seemed to influence their movements, since they always gave the impression of being a little stiff. Except for one who did not reach even as far as my chin, they were all of my height. They all seemed equally strong, but again not so much so that I would have been afraid of them. Singly and in the open, I would have been a match for any of them.

After an eternity a noise from the door wrenched me from my thoughts. I turned round and saw a woman coming slowly towards me. She was stark naked and barefoot just like me. I was speechless, and she seemed to be amused by my expression. She was very beautiful, quite unlike the women I know. Her hair was soft and blonde, almost platinum blonde – as if bleached – and curled inwards at the ends, down the nape of her neck. Her hair was parted in the middle and she had large, blue eyes, which were almond-shaped. Her nose was straight. Her face was unusually shaped with exceptionally high cheekbones; much broader than the South American Indian women. Her pointed chin made her face almost triangular. She had thin, unobtrusive lips, and her ears, which I did not see until later, were exactly like those of our women. She had the most beautiful body which I have ever seen on a woman, with high, well-shaped breasts and narrow waist. She was broad in the hips, had long thighs and small feet, narrow hands and normal finger-nails. She was much smaller than I am, and her head only reached to my shoulder.

This woman came silently up to me and looked at me as if she wanted something from me. Suddenly she put her arms around me and began to rub her face against mine. At the same time she pressed her body against me. She had the white skin of our blonde women and arms which were covered with freckles. I only noticed her typically feminine smell, but no other perfume on her skin or in her hair.

· The door had closed again. Alone with this woman, who clearly gave me to understand what it was she wanted, I became very excited. That sounds very improbable given the situation I was in, but I think that the fluid with which I had been rubbed was responsible for it. They must have done it on purpose. I only know that I could no longer control my sexual excitement. That had never happened to me before. Finally I forgot everything, seized the woman and responded to her caresses. It was a normal act, and she behaved like any other woman – even after repeated embraces. Finally she became tired and was breathing heavily. I was still excited, but now she withheld herself from me. When I noticed this I sobered up. So that was what they wanted me for – as a stud horse to bring fresh blood to their stock. I was somewhat annoyed by this, but put a good face on it, as I had after all had a thoroughly pleasant experience. But I would not like to exchange her for one of our women, for I prefer a woman with whom one can talk and who understands one. I was also irritated by the grunting sounds she made at particular moments. Apparently she did not know how to kiss either, unless her playful bites on my chin had the same meaning. But I am not so sure about this. The hair under her armpits and 'that in another place' was, unusually, red, almost blood red. Shortly after we had parted from one another, the door opened and one of the men called the woman to him. Before she went out she turned round once more and pointed first at her belly, then with a kind of smile at me and finally at the sky – in a southerly direction, I think. Then she went out. I understood this gesture as a warning that she would come back and take me there with her, wherever it might be. I still tremble at the thought today, for if they come back and take me again I am lost. I would not be separated from my family and my homeland for anything.

Then one of the men came back with my clothes under his arm, and I got dressed again. Apart from my lighter, nothing was missing. It could have been lost in the struggle. We went back into the other room, where three of the crew members were sitting on the swivelling stools and grunting to one another (I think they were conversing). Those who had fetched me went over to them and just left me standing. While they were 'talking' to one another, I tried to record every detail in my mind exactly and observe everything. In doing so I noticed a rectangular box with a glass lid on the table by the men. Inside was a disc which resembled the face of an alarm clock. There was one hand, and in place of the three, six and nine there were black markings. Only in the place where the twelve is normally were four small black signs close together. I do not know what for, but that is how they were.

At first I thought the instrument must be a kind of clock, because one of the men glanced at it from time to time. But that cannot have been so, since although I looked at it for quite a long time, the hand did not move its position.

Then it occurred to me to grab the object, as I needed some proof of my adventure. With this box my problem would have been solved. If these men noticed my interest in it they might perhaps decide to give it to me. I cautiously moved closer and closer to it, while the men were not looking at me, and then quickly snatched the instrument from the table with both hands.

It was very heavy and weighed more than two kilos. But I did not even have time to look at it more closely, for one of the men immediately sprang to his feet, thrust me aside, angrily tore the box from my hands and returned it to its place.

I retreated to the nearest wall and stood there motionless. I am not afraid of anyone, but in this case I preferred to remain quiet. For it could turn out that they would only treat me amiably if I behaved properly. So why should I take a risk which in any case held no hope of success. So I simply remained standing and waited.

I did not see the woman again, either naked or dressed. But I did discover where she must be. In the front part of the large room there was another door; it was not quite shut and I noticed footsteps going to and fro behind it from time to time. As all the others were with me in the room itself, it could only have been the footsteps of the woman. I suspect that this front part was the navigation area of the machine, but naturally I cannot prove it.

Finally one of the men stood up and gave me to understand that I should follow him. The others took no notice of me, and we ran through the small ante-room to the exterior door which was open with the ladder already lowered. We did not go down, however, and it was indicated that I should come on to the platform which there was on either side of the door. It was quite narrow, but one could walk round the machine on it in either direction. First we went to the front, and I saw a rectangular metal projection which stuck out from the machine – there was exactly the same thing on the opposite side. I concluded from the shape that it might control the take-off and landing of the machine. I must admit that I never saw this part in motion, even when the machine was taking off. So I cannot explain its meaning or function.

At the front the man pointed to the metal spikes – or rather metal spurs – which I have already mentioned. All three were firmly joined to the machine, the central one directly to the nose. They were all the same shape, tapering from a broad base to a fine point, and stood out horizontally. I cannot judge whether they were of the same metal as the machine. They shone like glowing metal, but did not radiate any heat. A little above them were reddish lights. The two at the sides were small and round, while that at the front was gigantic. This was the front search-light which I have already described. Above the platform there were numerous rectangular lamps running round the machine, let into its hull. They shed a reddish glow on the platform. This ended at the front in a large, thick pane of glass which was deeply embedded in the metal, somewhat raised and tapered towards the side. As there were no other windows anywhere, this panel must have been used to look out through, although this must have been difficult, since the glass appeared very cloudy from the outside.

I think the spurs on the nose must have had something to do with the propulsive energy, since their lights became very intense when the machine was taking off and merged completely with the light from the main headlight.

After inspecting the front part of the machine we went aft again (this part was arched to a greater degree than the front), but before this we stopped and the man pointed up to where the gigantic plate-like dome was rotating above us. While it turned slowly, it was constantly bathed in greenish light, the source of which I could not make out. In conjunction with this there was a kind of whistling, which sounded like the noise of a vacuum cleaner, or as if air were being sucked through numerous small holes.

When the machine took off later, the dome began to rotate faster and faster, until it could no longer be seen and only a bright red glow remained.

At the same time the noise increased to a loud howling, and I realized that the speed of rotation of the dome was directly connected with the noise. When I had seen everything, the man finally brought me to the metal ladder and gave me to understand that I could now go. When I was standing on the ground again I looked up once more. The man was still standing there, and he pointed first at himself, then down at me and finally heavenwards in a southerly direction.

The metal step ladder retracted, the steps closed into one another like a pile of planks and when the latter had come up, the door – which had formed the ramp when it was opened – was raised until it had fitted invisibly into the side of the machine again. The light from the lamps over the metal spurs, the main headlight and the dome got brighter and brighter as the latter's speed of rotation increased. Slowly the machine climbed vertically upwards, and at the same time the three-legged landing gear retracted like a tripod into the floor of the machine, and afterwards the underside of the flying object looked as smooth as if there had never been any undercarriage.

The flying object slowly went on rising until it was thirty to fifty metres above the ground. There it remained for a few seconds while the intensity of the light increased. The humming grew louder and the dome began to turn at breakneck speed, its light constantly changing until it was bright red. At that moment, the machine leaned slightly to one side, a rhythmic knocking sound could be heard, and suddenly it shot away in a southerly direction. In a few seconds it was already out of sight.

I now went back to my tractor. I had been dragged into the alien machine at 1.15 a.m. and I had now left it again at 5.30 in the morning. So they had held me there for four and a quarter hours. A long time.

I have told no one apart from my mother of my experience. She said it is better to have nothing more to do with such people. I did not dare to say anything about it to my father. I had already told him about the light on the dome, but he did not believe me and declared that I had simply imagined everything.

Later I decided to write to Senhor João Martins. In November I had read his article in the *Cruzeiro*, in which he invited his readers to inform him about all incidents connected with flying saucers. If I had had enough money I would have come to Rio sooner. But I had to wait until he informed me that he would meet part of the cost of the journey.

Clinical notes and report on medical investigation by Dr Olavo Fontes

Subject: Antônio Villas Boas, white, single, farmer.
Place of Residence: São Francisco de Sales in the state of Minas Gerais.

Medical report

As is apparent from his statement, he left the machine on 16 October 1957 at 5.30 a.m. He was in a weakened state as he had eaten nothing since 9 o'clock the previous evening, and had vomited several times in the machine. He returned home exhausted and slept almost throughout the day. When he awoke at 4.30 p.m. he felt well and ate a normal meal. But both on this night and the following nights he could not get any sleep. He was nervous and very excited; he did manage to doze off several times, but he immediately dreamed about the events of the previous night, as if he were experiencing the whole thing over again. Each time he awoke in a panic and again had the feeling of being seized and taken prisoner by aliens.

After this had happened several times, he gave up his vain attempts and instead decided to spend the night in study. But he did not succeed in this either, since he was in no state to concentrate on what he was reading. His thoughts returned continually to the events of the previous night. By daybreak he was completely shattered, running to and fro and smoking one cigarette after another. He was tired and felt completely exhausted. He needed to eat something, but he only drank a cup of coffee. Directly after this he became ill, and nausea and unbearable headaches continued throughout the day. Since he suffered from a complete loss of appetite, he was unable to contemplate taking any food.

He spent the second night also without sleep and in an unchanged state. He felt an unpleasant burning in his eyes, but the headaches had stopped.

On the second day he again had to fight against nausea and loss of appetite, but no longer vomited, possibly because he had not eaten. The burning in his eyes had got worse, however, and his eyes began to water continuously. However, there was no sign of any swelling of the conjunctiva or any other irritation of the eyes, nor was his vision affected. On the third night the patient was able to sleep and spent a normal night. But from this point onwards he experienced an excessive need for sleep for about a month. He continually dozed off even during the day, no matter where he was and even in the course of conversations with other people. As soon as he remained still for a short time he went to sleep. During this period of somnolence, the burning and excessive watering of the eyes also persisted. When the nausea ceased on the third day, his appetite also returned and he could once more eat normally. He discovered the state of his eyes worsened in the sun, and that he was obliged to avoid bright light. On the eighth day he injured himself slightly on the forearm at work and drew blood. On the next day he noticed that the wound had become inflamed, had a small pustule and itched violently. When this wound had healed, a red circle was left behind. Some four to ten days after this, similar skin blemishes appeared without prior injury on the forearms and legs. They began with a pustule open in the middle, which itched violently and only healed after ten to twenty days. He mentioned that after they had dried these pustules remained dark red round the edges and left scars.

He denied suffering otherwise from herpes or inflammations of the skin. Nor had he noticed any haemorrhages, bruises or minor lesions; if they had occurred, they had not come to his attention. He did mention, however, that on the fifteenth day after his experience two yellowish, more or less symmetrically formed discolourations appeared on either side of his nose. 'The places seemed pallid, as if they were not being properly supplied with blood,' he said. But after about ten days they disappeared as suddenly as they had come. Apart from the scars left by the pustules, which have recurred sporadically over the past few months, there are still two small open places on his arms. The other symptoms described have not so far reappeared. At the moment he feels well and judges his general state of health as good.

He denies having suffered from any of the following symptoms during the acute phase of his illness or in connection with it: fever, diarrhoea, haemorrhages, jaundice. He did not notice any peeling of the skin on the body or face, nor has he observed any excessive loss of hair between October and the present day. During the period of somnolence, there was no noticeable diminution of his capacity for work. Nor did he notice any diminution in his sex drive or potency, or in his powers of vision. No anaemia, no mouth ulcers.

Medical history
Among the acute children's illnesses he mentioned only measles and chicken-pox. No complications. Sexual diseases negative. In the past he has suffered from colitis, which currently does not give him any trouble.

Medical examination
The subject is a person of the male sex; white; soft, black hair, dark eyes.

No visible acute or chronic infirmities to be found.

Appearance: Atypical,* medium size (1.64m in shoes), slender but powerful, well developed musculature.

Nutritional state good; no sign of vitamin deficiency; no malformations or physical anomalies.

Bodily hair and sexual characteristics: no distinguishing features.

Teeth: well preserved.

Ganglia: not distinguishable from the exterior.

Mucous membranes: somewhat pale overall.

Dermatological examination
The following changes were noted:

1. Right and left of the chin two small, hyperchromic, almost round patches; one of them the size of a Brazilian ten-centavo piece, the other somewhat larger and more or less irregular in outline. At these places the skin appears thinner and more tender, as if it had only recently been formed, or was somewhat atrophied. There are no clues to the age and origin of these two marks. All that can be said is that they are the scars of superficial wounds, caused by blood-letting, which were produced at the earliest twelve months and at the latest one month previously. It can be assumed that these are merely skin blemishes which will probably have disappeared again in a few months. Otherwise no similar blemishes or marks were discovered.
2. Several recently produced scars (a few months old at the most)

of skin wounds on the backs of the hands, the forearms and the legs. Examination revealed that these are small scarred pustules or wounds with a scaly peripheral area. From this it can be deduced that they are only of recent origin. Two of these pustules on the right and left arm are not yet healed. They take the form of small, reddish, raised spots or boils, feel harder than the surrounding skin, are sensitive to pressure and secrete a yellowish, serous fluid in the centre. The surrounding skin is inflamed. Scratch marks from the patient's finger-nails suggest that they are a pruriginous eruption.

In respect of these skin changes the following should be mentioned: all apparent scars and skin blemishes are surrounded by a purplish red hyperchromic zone – a feature which lies completely outside our field of experience. Thus no judgement can be given as to whether these zones are of special importance. As we are not specialists in dermatology, we are not in a position to interpret them with sufficient certainty. We have therefore restricted ourselves to a description of the blemishes, which have also been photographically recorded.

Investigation of neurological state

Space and time orientation: good.

Emotional reactions, affections: within the norm.

Testing of spontaneous and deliberately stimulated attention: within the norm.

Testing of perceptive ability; mental association and intelligence tests: normal reactions.

Long- and short-term memory: good.

Visual memory: exceptional; details verbally described by the patient can be sketched or drawn without difficulty.

There is a complete lack of any direct or indirect signs which might indicate mental illness.

Testified by Olavo Fontes, M.D.,
Rio de Janeiro, 22 February 1958.

Summing up, Dr Fontes repeated that Boas had no psychopathic tendencies, and had been lucid from the beginning. He had not shown a single sign of confusion during his account, neither contradicting himself nor losing his self-control. His occasional hesitations were entirely congruent with the behaviour of a man who simply has no answer to questions arising from unusual circumstances. At such moments he would answer: 'I don't know that', or: 'I can't explain that' – even when it was obvious to him that any uncertainty on a particular question would cast doubts on his veracity.

Boas had also told the journalist João Martins that he had found it painful to talk about certain details, meaning of course the experience with the woman. He showed great reluctance in relating this intimate episode, and it was only with some persistence that the journalist succeeded in getting the exact details out of him.

Emotional utterances of this kind are entirely what one might expect from a psychologically normal person of his origin and upbringing.

Boas was in no way superstitious or mystically inclined, and he did not regard the U.F.O.'s crew members as angels, supermen or demons. On the contrary, he accepted that they were men, albeit from some other region or planet than our own. He explained that he believed this because the crew member who had led him out of the flying object had pointed first at himself, then at the ground and finally somewhere up at the sky. He deduced from the fact that the crew members spent the whole time in sealed suits and helmets that the air they were used to must be different from that on earth.

When the journalist João Martins told him that in the event of the report being published many people would regard him merely as a madman or a swindler, Boas was not in the least impressed. He answered: 'I would invite anyone who made such insinuations to my home and ask them to investigate my background. They would soon discover whether I am considered an honourable man there or not.'

Naturally, Martins was quite correct in thinking that many people would take Boas for an unfortunate lunatic. But assuming that Boas had intentionally invented such a fantastic fairytale, the question would remain of why he had done so. The financial advantages could not entirely be discounted, but it later transpired he was not in the least interested in them. He could not even count on his story arousing public interest, with all the attention he might expect to receive from this, for Martins had left him in no doubt from the start that he would not be able to publish his account. (The Brazilian secret service forbade press coverage of the case for a long time.)

Another possibility was that his story was the result of an inferiority complex or some form of sexual repression. However, this had already been excluded by Dr Fontes in his psychological report. Boas was certainly shy and hesitant, but there was no evidence that he was repressed or complex-ridden. Today he is happily married and lives on his farm with his wife and children. He still maintains that the incident took place exactly as he described it, and otherwise does not wish to hear anything more about it.

Boas was not a drug addict.

U.F.O.s have always been an important subject in South America, and there have been innumerable reports of sightings. It can therefore be assumed that Boas already had some knowledge of the subject. Could it perhaps be that the incident was a product of his imagination, which became a subjective reality for him?

If this were the case, we would have to admire the imaginative powers of this simple Brazilian farmer, though the possibility of some kind of hallucination cannot of course be ruled out.

However that may be, there is one important factor which we have not yet mentioned, and which it is impossible to reconcile with a case of deliberate deception. Both Dr Fontes and other doctors, including the specialist Dr Walter Bühler from Rio de

Janeiro, stated categorically that the cause of Boas's symptoms was exposure to radioactivity. There was only one possible explanation for this – that he had been near a source of radiation. Here was an effect which not even the liveliest imagination could produce.

On 24 May 1978 I had the following conversation with one of the doctors who examined Boas at the time – Dr Walter K. Bühler, who lives in Rio.

BUTTLAR.   This is Johannes von Buttlar, speaking from Germany. I am sorry to telephone you like this, Dr Bühler, but I would like to ask you a few more questions about the Boas case.

BÜHLER.   Of course, go ahead.

BUTTLAR.   My first question is, do you think that Antônio Villas Boas was really telling the truth?

BÜHLER.   Yes, absolutely.

BUTTLAR.   Second question: Do you also believe, Dr Bühler, that it was a real experience for Boas, or was it perhaps something which he imagined, which then became a reality for him?

BÜHLER.   For me there is not the slightest doubt that it was a real occurrence.

BUTTLAR.   Now my third and last question: it is said that Boas had been exposed to radioactivity. Is that true?

BÜHLER.   It has not so far been made public that Boas was examined by Dr Fontes with a Geiger counter, and distinct signs of background radiation were found on him.

BUTTLAR.   At the U.F.O.'s landing place?

BÜHLER.   No, no. On the man himself. In any case the sighting was confirmed to me by Boas's brother when I visited him at the farm.

BUTTLAR.   Thank you very much, Dr Bühler.

10

Absolutely Authentic

Even if the Boas case in itself had not been enough to call the Brazilian Secret Service on to the scene, there were two further incidents which seemed to require their serious consideration.

In the early hours of the morning on 3 November 1957, two sentries at the heavily defended Brazilian fort of Itaipu near Santos were going their rounds when one of them suddenly noticed an orange light over the sea. To his amazement it became larger and larger and was obviously approaching the fort. The sentry's initial surprise turned to fear as the object loomed steadily larger in the darkness. It soon became obvious to him that this was no ordinary phenomenon. The object held its course until it was directly over the sentries, and was visible as a gigantic round flying body which flooded the ground and the guns with a mysterious red light. The sentries gazed up at the threatening monster with open mouths – its diameter was at least as large as the wingspan of a DC-3 and scarcely a hundred metres away. Suddenly there was a strange buzzing noise, and the men simultaneously felt a wave of glowing heat. One of them collapsed on the spot, but the other succeeded in reaching safety in the shadow of one of the gun emplacements. His shouts of alarm roused his comrades inside the fortress, where the lights suddenly went out. Men ran to and fro in confusion, tumbling out into the open to bring help to the sentry. In the meantime the emergency electricity supply had been switched on, but immediately gave out.

Only a few minutes after the sentries' first cries for help two men were out of the fort and at their sides. They too saw the U.F.O., which was by now flying back across the sea. Although it no longer loomed directly over them as it had over the sentries, its luminous presence seemed real enough as it shot away across the Atlantic.

The sentries both had to be taken to hospital in Rio, where they remained under observation for some time. They had both suffered second- and third-degree burns on large areas of their body, and strangely enough these were chiefly on the parts which had been covered by their clothing.

On 16 January 1958, the Brazilian marine research vessel *Almirante Saldanha* was stationed off the minuscule island of Trinidade in the South Atlantic, taking part in a project connected with the International Geophysical Year. For the purpose of the International Geophysical Year, the Brazilian government had turned this former Second World War naval base into a meteorological and oceanographic research station.

The marine research ship had been in the area since the beginning of January 1958, and on 16 January it was standing off Trinidade, ready to put out to sea. There were 300 people on board including the crew. Among them was a retired officer of the Brazilian Air Force, Captain J.T. Viegos, a professor of geology named Fernando, various highly qualified marine researchers and scientists, and also an expert in underwater photography, Almiro Barauna.

Shortly before midday, when the *Almirante Saldanha* was due to weigh anchor, Barauna was taking a few last photographs with his Rolleiflex when the ship suddenly resounded with shouts of '*Oh lá, o disco*', and he saw a greenish luminous disc in the sky, which must have been about twenty-five feet high and about 130 feet in diameter. Everyone watched as the object crossed the island from the east, made directly for Desjado Peak, turned abruptly and hurtled off in a north-easterly direction,

Barauna had quickly raised his camera and taken a couple of shots before the object disappeared. After a few seconds it swept round in a curve and came back again. This time Barauna managed to take some closer snapshots of the Saturn-shaped object, which came out a great deal larger than before. Altogether he took six pictures, of which the first two were overexposed, the third came out perfectly, the fourth and fifth failed to catch anything in the general mêlée, but the sixth once again showed the mysterious disc clearly, before it finally disappeared over the sea.

After an exhaustive analysis of these pictures and negatives by the Brazilian Navy's photographic evaluation laboratories, they were finally published as absolutely genuine with the agreement of President Juscelino Kubitschek himself.

The official report of Admiral of the Fleet and Chief of Naval High Command Antonio Maria de Carvalho (secret document no. 0098/M-20) contains the following observations:

From paragraph I-V:

Finally another U.F.O. alarm was recorded on 16 January 1958 at 12.15. This time on board the *Almirante Saldanha*, which was anchored off the island of Trinidade. The ship was on the point of departure, and crew members were just hauling the pinnace used for shore trips on board when a U.F.O. alarm was given simultaneously from the bows and stern.

From paragraph I-VI:

A civilian professional photographer, who was among those

on board, and was photographing the hauling in of the boat, was alerted and was able to take the four attached photographs.

From paragraph I-VII:

After the sighting, Barauna took the film out of the camera in the presence of Lieutenant Commander Carlos Alberto Bacellar and other officers. Later he was accompanied by Bacellar to the photographic laboratory on board the research vessel. The film took only ten minutes to develop and the negative was examined by Bacellar immediately afterwards. He made a sworn statement that he checked the strip of negative while it was still wet, and that he recognized the U.F.O. in question on it.

From paragraph I-VIII:

Concurrently the negatives in question were shown to members of the ship's crew who had been eyewitnesses of the phenomenon. They confirmed that the object which appeared on the photograph was identical with the one which they had observed in the air.

With the agreement of the Brazilian naval ministry, the following statement by Lieutenant Commander Bacellar was issued to the press:

1. An unidentified flying object was actually observed by a number of people on the deck of the *Almirante Saldanha*. I myself did not witness the sighting, as I was in my cabin at that moment. However, I was called to the bridge directly afterwards.
2. The incident naturally aroused a great deal of excitement, and many people ran on deck, alerted by the shouts of the eyewitnesses.

3. The professional photographer, Almiro Barauna, was on deck with his camera and was in a state of nervous exhaustion after the incident. I remained at his side the whole time, as I wanted to be present when the film was being developed.

4. As soon as Barauna had recovered sufficiently – about an hour after the incident – the film was developed in the ship's laboratory . . .

5. Retired Air Force Captain José Theobaldo Viegos watched the developing of the film attentively with a pocket lamp in his hand, while I stood outside. I saw the newly developed film while it was still wet, and after careful examination came to the conclusion: that the course of this object's flight matched the scenery which Barauna had photographed from the ship shortly before the occurrence . . .

6. As previously agreed, I later went to see Barauna in Rio and accompanied him twice to the Naval Ministry.

7. I pointed out to him that he would not be allowed to publish the photographs without official permission, and told him that he would be notified as soon as the appropriate authorities had agreed to their publication.

8. Barauna left the negatives at the Naval Ministry and later received them back via me. On this occasion I told him that – with some restrictions – he could do as he thought fit with the photographs.

9. At my instigation and using the photographic paper which had been supplied by me, Barauna printed six complete series of the four pictures and made sixteen enlargements of details of the flying objects.

10. This event brought the number of confirmed sightings of unidentified flying objects over the island of Trinidade to four within forty days.

On 24 February 1958 the Navy Minister, Admiral Alves Camera, made the following statement to United Press in Petropolis: 'The Brazilian Navy is involved in an important secret which cannot be made public, since there is no explanation for it. I have not believed in flying saucers until now, but Barauna's photographic proof has now convinced me.'

On the same day, Commander Moreira da Silva said:

I do not wish to question the integrity of the photographer who snapped the unidentified flying object. It was observed by a series of authoritative witnesses. I can in any case verify that the photos are authentic and that the film was developed immediately on board the *Almirante Saldanha* – moreover that the negative was immediately examined by a number of different officers and not, as has been suggested, only eight days later. Any possibility of a photographic forgery was completely excluded.

From an analysis of the negative and the details reported by the numerous eyewitnesses, experts were able to estimate the speed of the flying object at a minimum of 750 m.p.h., and considerably higher when it accelerated.

It was not until later that it was discovered that the research vessel's entire electrical system had failed when the U.F.O. appeared.

Whatever our attitude towards flying saucers, the fact remains that this incident was not only recorded on film but also confirmed in writing by forty-eight eyewitnesses who were on deck at the time.

11

Turning Point

In the middle of April 1959, Jessup got in touch with Dr Manson Valentine, oceanographer and archaeologist and a friend of long standing. He told him that he wanted to talk to him about some new information relating to the Philadelphia Experiment, which he had written up in the form of a rough draft. Dr Valentine promptly invited Jessup to dinner on 20 April, but Jessup did not appear.

It was on 20 April, at approximately 6.30 p.m., that Morris K. Jessup was found dead in his car.

Many thousands of miles from there, on the outskirts of the small Australian town of Seymore, where there is an army camp, a commercial traveller named Jonathan Rainsfort watched from his car as a gigantic silver disc slowly descended from the sky. It suddenly stopped about 1300 feet above him, hovered there for a few minutes, then flew off at a fantastic speed.

'I was always convinced that U.F.O.s were a load of rubbish,' Rainsfort said later, 'but now things have changed. The question is, where did the thing come from, and what could it have been?'

Jessup had been convinced that he knew the answer – but now he was dead. He had spent a large part of his life in pursuit of one of life's great mysteries, and it was a mystery of which his death seemed to form a part. The official verdict was suicide caused by depression. But some of his friends were sceptical: 'He knew too much; they wanted him out of the way.' While the Air Force had vainly attempted to stem the rising tide of public accusations of dirty dealing by the publication of their Project Blue Book Special Report No. 14, Jessup's death merely added oil to the flames. The Air Force's Report 14 (one wonders what happened to Report 13) represented a major contribution to the U.F.O. theme. It took the form of a statistical analysis and computer evaluation, carried out by the Battelle Memorial Institute, and was undoubtedly an important piece of U.F.O. research. The study included 240 diagrams and maps incorporating detailed reports of U.F.O. sightings classified according to geographical location and other essential data.

One object of the study was to discover through computer analysis whether flying saucers represented an unknown technological development. It was also intended to discover any similarities in the motion and other characteristics of U.F.O.s and it was hoped to produce a model U.F.O. design.

Having been investigated for particular features by computer analysis, the U.F.O. reports were subsequently divided into groups and classified as: outstanding, good, mediocre and doubtful. A third of the reports fell into the 'outstanding' category – these cases representing genuine unidentified flying objects, for which there was simply no explanation.

Under this classification, the following incident undoubtedly qualifies as 'outstanding', since it has remained unexplained to this day. Although the episode has already been described in my book, *Time-Slip*, I could hardly leave it out here.

At the end of June 1959 on the island of New Guinea, more

precisely in the missionary area of the Anglican church of Boainai in Papua, an encounter took place which was to remain engraved in the participants' memories for many years to come.

The head of the mission at the time was the Reverend William Bruce Gill, who had graduated at Brisbane University in Australia. He kept a notebook in which the events of 27 and 28 June 1959 were described in every detail.

He was just about to go into the house when he saw a gigantic light in the sky towards the west. He said: 'I didn't think, of course, even then of flying saucers as such. I thought, well perhaps some people could imagine these things, but never me.'

The Reverend Gill called to mission member Eric Kodawara, showed him the light in the sky and asked him: 'What do you see up there?'

Only to receive the laconic reply: 'There seems to be a light.'

Gill sent Kodawara to fetch teacher Steven Moi and when Moi saw the light he immediately called together all the mission staff who could be found. They all stood staring in amazement at the sky and finally went up to the playing field, which was on higher ground, in order to get a better view.

Meanwhile Gill had got someone to fetch his notebook and a pencil, prompted by the thought that: 'If anything is going to happen, it's going to happen now, and surely tomorrow I'll wake up and think that it's been a dream, that I haven't really seen one. If I've got it down here in pencil, then I'll know at least I haven't been dreaming.'

And this is what the Reverend Gill wrote in his notebook:

Time 6.45 p.m. sky: patches of low clouds. Sighted bright white light, direction north-west. 6.50 called Steven and Eric. 6.52 Steven arrived confirms, not star. 6.55 send Eric to call people. One object on top moving – man. Now three men – moving, glowing, doing something on deck. Gone. 7.00 men 1 and 2 again. 7.04 gone again. 7.10 sky: cloud ceiling covered sky height about 2,000 feet. Man 1, 3, 4, 2, (appeared in that order) thin electric blue spotlight. Men gone, spotlight still there. 7.12 men 1 and 2 appeared blue light. 7.20 spotlight off, men go. 7.20 U.F.O. goes through cloud. 8.28 clear sky here, heavy cloud over Dogura. U.F.O. seen by me overhead. Called station people. Appeared to descend, get bigger. 8.29 second U.F.O. seen over sea – hovering at times. 8.35 another over Wadobuna Village. 8.50 clouds forming again. Big one stationary and larger. Others coming and going through clouds. As they descend through cloud, light reflected like large halo on to cloud – no more than 2,000 feet, probably less. All U.F.O.s very clear. 'Mother' ship still large, clear, stationary. 9.05 clouds patchy, numbers 2, 3, 4 gone. 9.10 number 1 gone overhead into cloud. 9.20 'Mother' back. 9.30 'Mother' gone, gone across sea toward Giwa. 9.46 overhead U.F.O. reappears, is hovering. 10.00 still stationary. 10.10 hovering, gone behind cloud. 10.30 very high hovering in clear patch of sky between clouds. 10.50 very overcast, no sign of U.F.O. 11.40 heavy rain.

Data sheet of observation of U.F.O.s 6.45–11.04 p.m.

Signed William B. Gill

The Reverend Gill also noted that men 1 and 2 appeared, followed by a blue light, at about 19.12. He estimated the height of the clouds by comparison with a nearby mountain. He relates that everything took place under the cloud cover, and that at this point the sky became overcast within twenty minutes. The U.F.O. had come through the cloud cover at 19.20. And the sky had cleared again at 20.28 despite the heavy cloud. It had remained overcast only over the village of Giwa. When Gill saw a U.F.O. there, he called the mission staff together for the second time that evening, since it was getting larger and seemed to him to be about to land. Other U.F.O.s also appeared and passed through the now broken cloud cover. They shot through the clouds, casting reflections on them from their lights, and then climbed upwards – 'They seemed to enjoy doing that,' Gill said.

On the following evening the U.F.O.s visited Boainai again, making an unforgettable impression on the mission staff.

Gill was taking a walk with some of his colleagues when one of the hospital sisters first noticed the object. It was about 6 p.m., earlier than on the previous evening. The U.F.O. 'was practically the closest we were ever to see it'. Dusk was falling, and the gleaming object was quite clearly to be seen. Right on top, 'on the decking', as Gill put it, there was once again a standing figure, who was joined by three others. Simultaneously, two other smaller objects appeared, one directly overhead and the other over the hills. The teacher Ananias said: 'I wonder if it is going to land on the playing field.'

The mission staff waved up at the ship as if waving to someone in greeting and received a waved greeting in return. Two young men from the mission now raised their arms above their heads and waved again. Once again their greeting was returned. The Reverend Gill relates that Ananias Rarata and himself now also waved, and the figures on the deck of the U.F.O. waved in return, much to the joy of the mission staff.

As darkness fell, Gill sent someone to fetch a pocket torch from the mission and sent repeated signals to the deck of the U.F.O. After a while it answered Gill's signals by moving backwards and forwards.

Thirty-eight witnesses observed this episode, and twenty-five of them, including five teachers and three medical assistants, signed the Reverend Gill's report.

These were not the only U.F.O. sightings over Papua at this period, as it is apparent from the notes of the Reverend Norman E.G. Cruttwell, who belonged to the Anglican mission in Menapi. The first report of a sighting in this period came from Papua's director of civil aviation, T.P. Drury.

The Reverend Gill wrote in connection with the events in Papua:

The Boainai sightings climaxed a relatively short but remarkably acute period of U.F.O. activity in the vicinity of east New Guinea. U.F.O.s were observed by both Papuan natives and Europeans. Sightings were reported by educated Papuans and by totally illiterate natives relatively untouched by Western civilization and quite ignorant of 'flying saucers'.

Professor Allen Hynek, currently director of the Lindheimer Astronomical Research Center at Northwestern University in the United States, takes the following view of the Boainai sightings:

I first learned of the case in detail when I stopped at the British Air Ministry on an official visit from Blue Book in 1961.

I learned at that time that the British military view of the U.F.O. problem was essentially the same as that of Blue Book; indeed, the British (and other governments as well) were looking to the U.S. Air Force to solve the problem. I was told quite bluntly that with the funds and facilities available to the U.S. Air Force there was little point to their doing anything about the problem, and they honestly felt that the U.S. Air Force was doing something about it, but with negative results . . . Since then I have had access to a full report on this case and have also been the recipient of a lengthy tape-recording of a talk by Reverend Gill and, more recently, of an hour-long tape with Reverend Gill made by my colleague Fred Beckman.

Before judgement is passed on this affair, Reverend Gill should be heard. As a few excerpts from his tapes show, Reverend Gill is utterly sincere. He talks in a leisurely, scholarly way, delineating details slowly and carefully. The manner and content of the tapes are conducive to conviction.

One would find it difficult to believe that an Anglican priest would concoct a story involving more than two dozen witnesses out of sheer intent to deceive. Critics of this case do not generally know that his report is only one of some sixty in the New Guinea area at approximately that time, all investigated by a colleague of Gill, the Reverend Norman Cruttwell, who has written a report covering the series, only one of which, the case in point, involved humanoids.

Fourteen days later the following episode took place in the Pacific, this time near Honolulu in the Hawaiian Islands.

On Saturday 11 July 1959, the crews of five different commercial airliners reported sighting a U.F.O. formation east of Honolulu. Panam Captain Wilson was on a night flight from San Francisco to Honolulu when, at 3.02 a.m. Hawaiian time, he noticed a large, bright light in the sky accompanied by some smaller ones. The airliner was flying at an altitude of about 23,000 feet and was over cloud cover when the object appeared about 1,000 feet above the machine and to the left.

> My co-pilot Richard Lorenz, and the flight engineer, Robert Scott, could not believe their eyes when the light rushed towards us. For some ten seconds it maintained its approach on a parallel course and would have comfortably passed to port of us if it had been another aircraft. But this object suddenly made a sharp turn at a speed at which no known aircraft type could have carried it out and simply disappeared. The smaller, evenly spaced lights seemed to be either part of a large object or to demonstrate damned good formation flying.

Wilson firmly excluded the possibility that the phenomenon was caused by reflected light. 'The night was pitch black,' he said.

The crews of five commercial aircraft in all observed the

object from four different positions, and all of them ruled out the possibility of any kind of reflection.

After landing in Honolulu, Wilson declared that in his nineteen years' experience of flying he had never seen anything like it, and had hitherto always doubted the existence of U.F.O.s. 'But now I'm convinced of it.'

The other airline captains also submitted reports; they were Captain Lloyd Moffat of Canadian Pacific Airways, First Officer Erwin Zedwick of Slick Airways, Captain Noble Sprunger and Captain E.G. Kelley, both of Pan American Airways.

Wilson's report was confirmed in every detail by Moffat, who said: 'I've never seen anything like it in my whole life. Five of us saw the thing at the same time.'

An Air Force spokesman stated that all five pilots would have to fill in questionnaires and there would be an inquiry about the sighting. The reports were subsequently sent both to the Air Force High Command for the Pacific in Honolulu and to the Defense Department in Washington.

Another incident which caused a great deal of excitement at the U.S. Air Force High Command occurred on 24 September 1959 and gave rise to one of the Air Force's greatest U.F.O. hunts to date. This incident found its way into the files of the N.I.C.A.P. and was published by Major Keyhoe.

At about 5 o'clock in the morning, shortly before sunrise, a gigantic U.F.O. was observed sinking slowly down from the sky near Redmond Airport, Oregon. The first man to sight it was patrolman Robert Dickson, who was driving a patrol car on the outskirts of town. He saw a large illuminated object falling from the sky, and at first thought it was a burning aircraft about to crash.

Dickson was completely dumbfounded when the object suddenly 'stood still' in the air about 200 feet above him, and he saw that it was disc-shaped. The U.F.O. remained motionless for a few minutes, then climbed vertically, flew over the airfield and stopped again at the north-eastern end. The patrolman drove straight to the airfield and mentioned the incident to air safety control officer Laverne Wertz.

Wertz and other members of the Federal Aviation Administration (F.A.A.) followed the saucer through field-glasses for some minutes. The bright light had become duller, and they could all clearly see strange yellow, red and green beams on the edge of the disc. At 5.10 a.m., Wertz sent a telex to the air safety control centre in Seattle, which was relayed directly to Hamilton Air Force base in California. Within minutes, the Air Force informed Seattle that interceptors were already on the way from Portland air base and the Air Force radar station at Klamath, Oregon, was following the object on its screens.

In Redmond, F.A.A. officials were still watching the object through their binoculars when they heard the whistle of the approaching jets. As soon as the fighters dived on the U.F.O. from above, the beams around the edge of the disc disappeared. At the same time a luminous beam shot out of its underside, catapulting the machine upwards at a fantastic rate so that it almost collided with the leading fighter. The next jet banked violently to avoid a collision and another was drawn into the slipstream of the rising U.F.O. so that the pilot almost lost control of his machine. Three other pilots climbed after the fleeing U.F.O., but despite using the additional thrust of their after-burners, were soon left behind. When the U.F.O. disappeared into the clouds at about 16,500 feet, one of the fighters followed with the help of its radar. Its approach must have been registered on board the U.F.O., since it immediately altered its course. This change of course was followed closely by the high-level radar at the Air Force radar station at Klamath Falls.

The pilots now gave up their hopeless pursuit, but radar observers continued to pick up the U.F.O. on their screens as it swept to and fro in a series of hair-raising manoeuvres between 6,000 and 60,000 feet.

No sooner had the pilots landed than, still shaken by their alarming experience, they were summoned to a Secret Service inquiry. When they had described their meeting with the U.F.O., they received strict orders not to talk about the episode, even with each other.

But the screaming of the jets as they dived from the sky had brought out the citizens of Redmond in force. A large number of them had seen a strange light in the sky as well as the fighters. The Air Force was naturally afraid that its attempt at catching a U.F.O. would be discovered, and hurriedly issued an explanation that the fighters had been on a routine reconnaissance flight and had been misled by false radar signals. The light in the sky was dismissed as the 'imagination of excited witnesses'.

Within hours, however, a new development once more threw the Air Force into excitement. For as soon as the High Command heard of the luminous 'exhaust' of the U.F.O. there were fears that it might be a form of nuclear propulsion. Wertz was now ordered by the F.A.A. in Seattle to make a reconnaissance flight in the region of Redmond, in order to investigate the atmosphere for abnormal radioactivity. Flying in a helicopter and using a Geiger counter, Wertz quartered the area at the different altitudes at which the U.F.O. had hovered. The results of his investigation were telexed to the Air Force, but were not published for a long while afterwards.

The A.T.I.C., on the other hand, published a statement which told a very different story, namely that after careful investigation and analysis no material proof had been produced that U.F.O.s either were spaceships, and thus represented a threat to national security, or could be considered of scientific significance.

It was further stated that U.F.O. projects were expensive,

represented an unproductive burden for the Air Force and brought nothing in return but unfavourable publicity.

Although the Air Force was now intent on shutting down the whole U.F.O. programme, it seemed unable to draw the logical consequence – which would have been to open its files and make it known that it was abandoning the project since further involvement was not worth the effort.

But here the problem of public relations began to raise its head. The Air Force was extremely sensitive to public opinion and regarded its conflict with civilian U.F.O. researchers as nothing less than a state of war. Every attack on its methods was a battle in that war. To declassify its own secret files, to defuse the U.F.O. campaign, or announce its shutdown in the face of attacks was too much like capitulation.

Such at least was the conviction which Professor David Michael Jacobs expressed in his book *The U.F.O. Controversy in America.*

The authorities' schizophrenic behaviour, and the number of violently conflicting stories given to the public could in fact have a perfectly simple explanation. After years of fruitless attempts to come to some concrete conclusions over the U.F.O. phenomenon, and after the failure of their attempts to capture a U.F.O., the military and other secret services had reached breaking point. They simply did not know what to do. They could not go back, nor could they start again from the beginning without losing face. For this would have meant giving up their camouflage tactics and their various secret resolutions. As they did not know how to proceed, they found themselves in a hopelessly entangled situation and issued confused and contradictory statements.

No doubt by this point they wished they had never heard of U.F.O.s, flying saucers and suchlike. But the U.F.O. phenomenon was very much alive – whether they liked it or not – and public pressure was growing.

There was one particularly amusing incident which did nothing to put people's minds at rest. The U.S. Naval secret service was alerted to the fact that a woman in Maine claimed to have been in contact with extraterrestrial beings. The Navy immediately brought in the C.I.A.

Normally these authorities would have simply ignored a contact story in which contact had been established by means of 'automatic writing'. But the story had already reached the Canadian government, who had promptly sent their U.F.O. expert, Wilbert Smith, to interrogate the woman at home.

The contactee went into a trance and produced data on the technical aspects of space travel which far exceeded her possible knowledge of the subject. As soon as the U.S. Navy were told of this they sent two officers to investigate. The woman succeeded in persuading one of the Naval officers to allow himself to be put into a trance in an attempt to make contact with the extraterrestrial beings; unfortunately the attempt was unsuccessful. Back in Washington the two Naval intelligence officers mentioned their experience to C.I.A. officials, and the C.I.A. immediately arranged for another seance with the same officer. Sixteen witnesses gathered in the C.I.A. offices to act as observers, and this time the Naval officer who was put into a trance claimed to have made contact.

The sixteen witnesses naturally demanded proof. The officer who was in a trance told them to look out of the window, where they would see a U.F.O. Three of the men ran to the window and to their amazement actually saw a U.F.O. in the sky. Two of the witnesses were C.I.A. officials, the third was a Naval intelligence officer.

At exactly the same time, the radar centre at Washington National Airport reported a failure of radar signals in the direction of the sighting.

Major J. Friend, the new chief of Project Blue Book, was informed of this incident by the C.I.A. and took part in later seances. He asked to be kept informed of new developments, but nothing more transpired.

Friend was of the opinion that both the Naval officer and the woman should be thoroughly examined in the parapsychological laboratories at Duke University.

The sighting itself was never investigated by Blue Book, and what the witnesses had actually seen remained for ever a puzzle. The C.I.A. did not take the incident itself seriously, though it paid more attention to the officers involved. At the C.I.A.'s instigation all those involved were given disciplinary transfers.

On the evening of 22 February 1960 the Pentagon put out a documentary television programme which surveyed U.F.O. research since 1947. The programme also dealt with the U.F.O. invasion of the year 1952 over the military restricted zones in Washington and around the Pentagon, and ended with an astounding statement. According to an official communiqué from the Defense Department, there could be no doubt of the reality of U.F.O.s, or that they had intelligent crews and were of extraterrestrial origin.

12

Is There Intelligent Life on Earth?

While the secret services were busying themselves with 'extra-terrestrials' – whether denying their existence or attempting to catch them, science was making its own contribution to ufology. At exactly 4 o'clock in the early morning silence of 8 April 1960, the radio astronomer Dr Frank Drake began his search for signals from the Cosmos.

The instrument which he and his colleagues used for this purpose was the radio telescope of Green Bank Observatory, on a broad plateau in the Appalachian mountains. They took bearings on the stars Tau Ceti and Epsilon Eridani, hoping to pick up signals from extraterrestrial intelligences at a wavelength of 210 mm. The radio telescope lies among the forest-clad mountain slopes of West Virginia, shielded from all Earthly noises. The eight antennae are among the largest in the world, giant dishes pointing towards the sky, an ear open to the Cosmos.

The 210 mm wavelength is that of natural radiation from hydrogen atoms, and is the one scientists consider most likely to be used as a transmission frequency by advanced civilizations.

And thus Project Ozma was launched – a romantic name which Drake had taken from the queen of the unattainably distant land of Oz created by the American writer, Frank Baum.

The idea of interplanetary communication was by no means new. The ancient Greek philosopher Thales of Miletus (636–546 BC) suggested that stars could be other worlds. His pupil Anaximander even represented the view that there are innumerable worlds, coming and going in an endless succession, and Plutarch (AD 46–125) was convinced that the Moon was a miniature version of Earth, with mountains and valleys inhabited by demons.

The possibility of making contact, however, was not considered until more recently. One of the most fantastic proposals in this respect was made by the famous mathematician and astronomer, C.F. Gauss (1777–1855), who wanted to make a gigantic triangle out of forest avenues in Siberia, in order to attract attention. Another astronomer, the Austrian J.J. von Littrow (1781–1840), preferred warmer climes, suggesting the digging of geometrically arranged canals in the Sahara Desert, which could be illuminated with kerosene at night. The Frenchman C. Gros even suggested a gigantic mirror, which would send signals produced by reflected sunlight to the 'men on Mars'.

When radio waves were discovered, ideas began to take a more realistic form. One of the first men who claimed to have received signals of interstellar origin was the outstanding genius Nikola Tesla (1856–1943), who was one of the pioneers in this field. Thomas Edison himself had a similar experience. But as they were both attacked and ridiculed by their sceptical colleagues, they kept silent.

For 1,500 long years the Christians retained the Earth as the centre of the Universe. Eventually they were forced to recognize the fact that the Earth revolves round the Sun, but even the Sun was established as a new centre to the Universe. This was an attitude which could not outlast the discovery that our Sun itself is no more than one star among thousands of millions in the galaxy. And that was not all, for our own galaxy, the Milky Way, is again no more than one among thousands of millions in the Universe.

The final illusion of our uniqueness was taken from ـs more than fifty years ago by the Harvard astronomer, Harlow Shapley, who proved that our Sun is not even at the centre of the Milky Way, as had hitherto been suggested. Shapley showed our solar system, unthinkably, where it belongs, in an insignificant suburb of the Milky Way, some 30,000 light-years from the centre. If we imagine the Sun as being the size of a marble, then the Earth would be a grain of sand about three feet away from it. The next star would then be another marble 150 miles away. Using this model, the next advanced, technological civilization would be perhaps 18,000 miles away.

The diameter of the Milky Way is 80,000 light-years – light travels at about 186,000 miles per second in a vacuum. Thus in a year it travels the inconceivable distance of about 6 million million miles.

The spiral galaxy which we have given the name of the Milky Way is roughly the shape of a flying saucer; the existence of its spiral arms was long suspected, but could not be proved until the advent of radio astronomy. Our solar system is situated at the edge of one of these spiral arms. It takes 225 million years to revolve once round the galactic centre.

In the Milky Way alone there are some 150,000 million stars with innumerable planets and their natural satellites. Undoubtedly these include a large number which are enveloped in an ecosphere capable of supporting life. Our neighbouring stars were long ago inspected for irregularities which might suggest the existence of dark planets orbiting round them, and as expected a whole series of these dark satellites were discovered.

Within a radius of sixteen light-years around the Sun, there are forty-seven known stars, among which are three white dwarfs – stars which have used up their nuclear energy – eight binary stars and two triple stars. Thus there are twenty-two stars in our immediate vicinity which could harbour life-supporting planets.

Those closest to the earth and the most favourable to life are Epsilon Eridani, Epsilon Indi and Tau Ceti, all between ten and eleven light-years away. Epsilon Eridani, at around eleven light-years is 'only' 66 million million miles away from us, a distance that is entirely insuperable in the current state of Earth technology. If we can imagine an Apollo spacecraft travelling that distance with a crew, the trip would be as ambitious as for a snail to try crawling a hundred times round the world.

Before the beginning of the Ozma Project, Drake had calculated that it would only be possible to receive signals from a planet orbiting one of these two stars if they were sent by a 1 million watt transmitter via a 200 metre reflector.

Strangely, perhaps, we always seem to assume that extraterrestrial civilizations (assuming that they exist) must be far superior to our own. But suppose we look at the situation from their point of view. If they were inferior to us, they would probably have no transmitting or receiving apparatus. But if they were that far in advance of us, we would probably be far too uninteresting for them to make contact with us. They would probably already have enough information about our level of development from receiving our television and radio programmes. The only civilization likely to make contact with us would be one at a similar level of development to ourselves; and in this case contact would be unlikely to take place since the technical facilities of both sides would still be too primitive – which seems to leave us back where we started.

Project Ozma's chances of success were in fact nil from the beginning, since the Green Bank radio telescope is simply not advanced enough for such an undertaking. Even so, it was only after 150 hours of continuous, intensive and unproductive listening that it was finally broken off.

In abandoning the project, Drake reflected that technology

on Earth has developed in a relatively short space of time. A civilization only needs a hundred years or so to pass from total ignorance in the field of electromagnetic communication to near perfection. Compared with the life of man, this is a long time, but in the cosmic time-scale it only represents one-hundredth of a millionth part of the life of a star system.

Thus on the cosmic time-scale, which is the only one which counts, a planet would pass from total ignorance to total knowledge in technology at one bound.

As soon as a civilization had reached such a stage of knowledge, it would be in a position to make the first contacts with similar civilizations over interstellar distances. Earth has already reached this stage, and there must surely be technologically developed civilizations on other planets.

Obviously the number of civilizations using radio waves must depend on the number of new civilizations which arise every year. An additional factor is the average life-span of intelligent civilizations which make use of electromagnetic communication. If they have a very short life-span, the chances of their making contact are obviously small. We ourselves seem in danger of destroying one another before our natural life has run its course.

Thus, according to Drake, the number of civilizations with which we could communicate in the Cosmos depends not on the number of existing planets, but on a far more important question, namely: 'Is there intelligent life on Earth?' (This question was inscribed on a wall in the London Planetarium, and underneath it a witty astronomer who worked there had written, 'Yes, but I'm only visiting.')

'Let us be optimistic and assume that this is so,' says Drake. 'Then there are also intelligent communities in the Universe.'

Our technology is so far advanced that we can now transmit or receive signals over a distance of up to a hundred light-years.

Additional devices such as space probes or moon bases can increase our range to several thousand light-years.

But this is only of use to us in searching for, i.e. receiving, signals. The time difference alone would stand in the way of two-way communication, since we would have to wait many thousands of years between messages.

Although we have not as yet received any demonstrable extraterrestrial messages, it is by no means impossible that the Milky Way is buzzing with interstellar conversations. The well known exobiologist (exobiology = extraterrestrial biology) Professor Carl Sagan of Cornell University puts it like this: 'We are like the inhabitants of an isolated valley in New Guinea who communicate with societies in neighbouring valleys by runner and by drum,' without knowing that 'all the while, a vast international cable and radio traffic passes over them, around them, and through them.'

Our communication range has been even further increased by the 330 m diameter radio telescope erected by Cornell University in a deep mountain valley near Arecibo in Puerto Rico.

The Russians have also commissioned a radio telescope solely for the purpose of listening for signals transmitted by extraterrestrial civilizations from fifty relatively near stars. The project is headed by Dr V. Troitsky, director of the Radiophysical Institute in Gorki.

But unless we know the definite source of such communications, and their exact frequency, wavelengths and transmission power, no search of this kind can be anything but an illusion. If we were to receive any such signals, it would be purely by chance.

The invention of the optical laser (light amplification by stimulated emission of radiation) and maser (microwave amplification by stimulated emission of radiation) has made a contribution in this field by providing new methods of communication. If a signal of several million joules (the joule is a unit of energy) were radiated through a 200 m reflector in one-second impulses on the 210 mm wavelength, they would be able to travel a distance of up to 1,000 light-years.

But there is one factor which nullifies the effectiveness of all our sophisticated technological methods of making contact with extraterrestrials, and that is the time barrier.

One possible means of overcoming this problem would be the use of telepathy as a means of interstellar communication.

In 1963, at the International Astronautical Congress in Paris, someone suggested telepathy as the quickest, cheapest and most effective means of communication – only to be met with loud laughter from the other participants.

In 1974, the celebrated atomic physicist, Professor John B. Hasted of Birkbeck College at London University, began some experiments in the field of psychokinesis and teleportation; he produced some sensational results, which were published in April 1978. Hasted used amongst other things a resistance gauge, which was connected to metal objects or introduced into the experimental object. For in Hasted's view one of the most important rules in all these experiments was that none of the experimental objects should be touched.

As a result of its molecular structure, every metal has its own electrical potential. If some psychokinetic effect causes a bending, stretching or fracture of the metal, thus altering its molecular structure, this inherent potential will also be altered; and this alteration will be registered by the resistance meter.

Hasted placed pieces of metal in hermetically closed glass containers and attempted to influence them psychokinetically so that they would bend, stretch, twist or break. The subjects he used were for the most part children, to exclude the possibility of professional tricksters getting into the experiments.

Hasted also examined the pieces of metal which were exposed to psychokinesis under the electron microscope and by spectral analysis. He discovered that atoms are moved or displaced by the process of psychokinesis. The atomic structure of the metal objects was thus altered by psychokinetic 'influence'.

In other experiments it proved possible to displace objects in space through psychic influence – in a word by teleportation. The results of these experiments were nothing short of sensational. On ten occasions, it proved possible to make metal objects disappear either completely or temporarily from inside the hermetically closed glass containers without damaging or forcibly opening the containers, or altering them in any other way. In this connection, Professor Hasted speaks of 'parallel spaces', which can be regarded as sub-universes. His experiments prove that there is such a thing as psychokinesis, and what is more teleportation, both on the atomic level and on the level of larger objects than atoms.

Similar experiments have also been carried out in England, in Canada, at Berkeley and Stanford Universities in the United States, and by Dr Crussard in France.

These experiments prove the existence of new methods of communication which lift barriers of our known space-time continuum. Could this also be the key to the interstellar journeys which seem to have been made by U.F.O.s?

Professor J.A. Wheeler, of Princeton University, one of the few real experts on Einstein's theory of relativity, speaks of a parallel space, a super-space, as he calls it. In his model of the Universe he proposes an amazing new method of bridging vast distances. Wheeler likens the Cosmos to a ring, the upper surface of which bears all the heavenly bodies, while the hole in the centre incorporates another universe – his so-called super-space.

These two worlds lie side by side. But unlike our Universe, super-space is timeless. Today, tomorrow, yesterday, before, afterwards – these words have lost their validity. There is neither time nor speed.

If this model were accurate, then super-space could serve as a short cut to other solar systems. One would be able to travel from one part of the Universe to another faster than the speed of light.

Spaceships would plunge into this super-space and emerge again at their destination in another solar system, back in the normal space-time dimension.

The question then arises of how to gain access to this super-space. There is a clue here – most probably the so-called 'black holes' are the entrances to this other dimension. Black holes are gravity wells produced by the total, catastrophic collapse of an oversized star. All matter and energy in the neighbourhood of one of these black holes disappears. But where does it go to? Perhaps into super-space?

Do U.F.O.s perhaps already use super-space in order to traverse otherwise unattainable astronomical distances? If this were the case, it would at least dismiss one of the arguments used by those who deny the possibility of extraterrestrial visitors.

13
Theta Reticuli 1

On 19 September 1961, thirty-eight-year-old postal worker Barney Hill and his forty-year-old wife Betty, who was a social worker, were driving along U.S. Highway 3 from the Canadian frontier, through the White Mountains towards Portsmouth, New Hampshire. They had decided on the spur of the moment to take a day off, and as the weather forecast had warned of a hurricane, they were driving through the night to get home before it. They made a stop in Colebrook, in northern New Hampshire and continued their journey at 10 p.m. At the speed they were travelling, they would normally have arrived home around 2.30 in the morning.

South of Lancashire, New Hampshire, they noticed an extremely bright star in the sky. At least they assumed it was a star. There was practically no traffic on the roads, and the moon was so bright that the Hills would have been able to drive without headlights. When the supposed star suddenly changed course and passed in front of the moon, they thought it must be a satellite. Betty Hill followed it curiously from the window of the car with a pair of binoculars. It got larger and larger and seemed to be following them.

The Hills stopped in order to get a better look at the object.

Betty said later that they had never seen anything like it. It was round and had every possible kind of winking light. Barney Hill suddenly felt uneasy and ran back to the car, calling to his wife.

They leaped into the car and Barney drove hell for leather from the spot, excitedly shouting to his wife to keep an eye on the object.

They both suddenly saw the object, which they described as being ten storeys high, hovering in the air over the highway. Betty made out two rows of windows one above the other and a red light on either side. Barney Hill now stopped and jumped out of the car. Betty remained in her seat, but Barney ran towards the object and watched through the binoculars as it prepared to land. Betty shouted to him anxiously to come back, but Barney remained frozen to the spot, watching as a kind of stairway slowly emerged from the machine. Finally he pulled himself together, ran back to the car and pressed the starter. At that moment the Hills heard a strange electrical buzzing, which made the whole automobile vibrate. They felt a prickling all over their bodies and began to feel dizzy. From this point on Barney and Betty Hill could not remember anything more. They came to at the sound of a new buzzing noise, different from the first. They drove on along the road, and everything seemed strangely still. A signpost indicated fifteen miles to Concord. They didn't think at first to wonder how they had got so far from Ashland, where their journey had been interrupted. But when they thought about it seriously, they realized that something was obviously very wrong. They had lost two and a half hours, which had simply vanished from their consciousness.

What happened during these two and a half hours?

Betty Hill clearly remembered that an unidentified flying object had suddenly appeared. She also had a constantly recurring dream in which a group of similarly clad men were blocking the road. This dream was constantly repeated, but Betty could not consciously remember the experience. Finally they turned to N.I.C.A.P.

When Barney developed a stomach ulcer in January 1964, they both decided to follow the advice of Walter Webb, a N.I.C.A.P. investigator, and apply to the famous Boston psychiatrist, Dr Benjamin Simon, for treatment.

Dr Simon decided to treat them by hypnosis, hoping that by gaining access to the subconscious, he would obtain some information about the missing two and a half hours. He hypnotized Barney and Betty Hill individually and imposed a memory block on both of them through hypnotic suggestion. This prevented them from exchanging any kind of information about their experience, or from discussing their statements with each other. The two of them now relived, under hypnosis, the bizarre incident which they had experienced during the missing two and a half hours.

The tape-recording made during the sessions revealed the following sequence of events.

They had left the highway and driven along a narrow road, where they were stopped by some men about five feet tall. They were grotesque and in some way different, but Betty could not say exactly how. Up to this point she had not been afraid, but when the car refused to start and three of the aliens opened the door on her side, she panicked.

Then one of them laid his hand on her eyes. She had the feeling of sinking into sleep, although she tried not to. With a last effort of will she struggled against this state, and saw that the men were standing in a circle around the Hills.

While they were pulling Barney, accompanied by Betty, up the steps, she cried: 'Wake up, Barney!'

At this, one of the aliens at Betty's side asked her in careful English: 'Is his name Barney?'

Betty refused to reply.

The Hills both stated independently that the men were wearing uniforms.

According to Barney's description, the leader was wearing a shining black coat with a black sash hanging down the left shoulder and a cap which gave him the air of a naval captain. Betty was particularly impressed by the almost black eyes, whose expression alarmed her. The aliens seemed to have no ears, and their skin had a greyish tinge. Betty thought that they must be human, or humanoid, beings.

Once on board the U.F.O., the Hills were separated. Betty remained in the first room, while Barney was taken into the next. Betty described the first room as like a slice of cake with the tip cut off, and all the walls, she said, gleamed with a blueish light.

The leader and another man, who turned out to be a doctor, led Betty to a white chair, on which she had to sit and undergo a thorough examination of her eyes, neck, nose, ears and teeth.

She then had to lie on an examination table. Hitherto all the examinations had been painless, but now the doctor produced a long, needle-like instrument which he tried to introduce into her navel to make a pregnancy test, as he explained to Betty. She tried in vain to prevent him, and wept with pain when he introduced the needle. At this the men looked at each other in astonishment, and the leader quickly laid his hand over her eyes, at which the pain momentarily ceased. Betty Hill said that she assumed from this that they had not hurt her intentionally. This test concluded Betty's examination, and she was told that she would merely have to wait for Barney.

When the doctor passed into the next room to deal with Barney, Betty talked to the leader and told him that if she went home and told people what had happened to her, no one would believe her unless she could take some kind of proof.

The leader asked Betty what she would like to have. She looked round, discovered a book with phonetic symbols in it and asked whether she might have it. The leader agreed with a smile.

At that moment the doctor came out of the next room with Barney's false teeth in his hand. He went up to Betty, opened her mouth and tried to remove her teeth. He failed, since Betty still had her own teeth, and there was general consternation among the aliens. Betty then explained that people lose their teeth sooner or later, for different reasons, but mostly in old age. But the concept of age apparently meant nothing to the aliens, and they were unable to understand Betty's explanation.

Now Betty in turn inquired where the aliens and their spaceship had come from, and the leader produced a three-dimensional star map which somehow opened out from the wall. He explained to her that the thick lines leading from one point to another represented permanent trade routes, the thin lines occasional communications routes, and the dotted lines expeditionary routes. Unfortunately the stars on the map did not have names and were therefore no more than a 'glance out of the window' as far as Betty was concerned.

The leader told Betty that she would find our Sun on the map, but she did not know where to look.

There were twelve stars altogether, represented by floating spheres which radiated light. The leader remained silent, however, on the question of their origin. In the meantime, Barney had reappeared.

Betty was overjoyed, because she thought they could now go, but then she heard the crew members arguing with one another.

The leader came back, went up to Betty and took the book away from her, saying that it had been decided they must forget everything.

Betty protested that she could not forget such an extraordinary experience and then suggested the aliens should visit Earth again when a meeting could be arranged with experts who would answer their questions about life here.

The alien explained to her, however, that the decision did not lie with him, and in any case they always knew how to find the people they needed.

Then, without another word, the aliens conducted the Hills back to their car, and the spaceship disappeared as quickly as it had come.

After careful analysis of the case, Dr Simon came to the

conclusion that the Hills had described the encounter as they
believed they had experienced it.

A major factor in his findings was the record of the hypnosis
session, a short extract from which is given here. Barney is being
questioned by both Dr Simon and Allen Hynek, who was also
present at the session.

HYNEK. Barney, you will remember everything clearly, and I
want you to tell me what is happening; you have just heard
the beep-beep-beep; I want you to tell me what it sounded
like, and then each of you just relive and tell me what is
happening as you are driving down the road.

BARNEY. Betty, it's out there – it's out there, Betty! Oh God,
this is crazy. I'm going across a bridge – I'm not on Route 3.
Oh, my! Oh, my! Oh, my! [Barney breathing very heavily.]
Oh, I don't believe it. There are men in the road. I don't
believe it. I don't want to go on. It can't be there. It's the
Moon.

DR SIMON. Go on, Barney. You remember everything clearly
– everything's clear.

BARNEY. I'm out of the car, and I'm going down the road into
the woods. There's an orange glow; there's something there.
Oh, oh, if only I had my gun; if only I had my gun [in an
excited, despairing tone]. We go up the ramp. I'd love to lash
out, but I can't. I'd love to strike out, but I can't. My emotions
– I got to strike out – I got to strike out!... My feet just
bumped, and I'm in a corridor. I don't want to go. I don't
know where Betty is. I'm not harmed. I won't strike out, but I
will strike out if I'm harmed in any way. I'm numb. I have no
feeling in my fingers. My legs are numb. I'm on the table!

DR SIMON. It's all right. You can stop there. You're on the
table, but you're quiet and relaxed and you just rest now until
I say, 'Listen, Barney.' You won't hear anything I'm saying
for a little while. Betty, what's going on?

BETTY. We're riding – Barney puts on the brakes, and they

squeal, and he turns to the left very sharply. I don't know why he's doing this. We're going to be lost in the woods. We go around a curve. [Pause.] Barney keeps trying to start it – it won't start. In the woods now they come up to us. There's something about the first man who's coming up. This is when I get frightened, and I gotta get out of the car and run and hide in the woods . . .

HYNEK. Have you ever seen anything before that even resembled this?

BETTY. No.

HYNEK. Was the moon shining down on it? Could you see the moon at the same time?

BETTY. It was a very moonlit night. It wasn't quite as clear as daylight, but I could see. It was on the ground, and there was like a rim around the edge.

HYNEK. Was it resting on legs or was it flat on the ground?

BETTY. The rim was a little bit above the ground, and there was a ramp that came down.

HYNEK. How big was it, Betty? Compare it to something you know, Betty, in size.

BETTY. I tried to think it . . .

HYNEK. How about a railroad car? Was it bigger than a railroad car or smaller than a railroad car?

BETTY. I can't picture the size of a railroad car. I would say if it landed out here on the street – let's see, it would go from the corner by the front of the house and it would go beyond the garage.

HYNEK. What were your thoughts as you came closer and closer to it?

BETTY. To get the hell out of there if I could.

HYNEK. And why couldn't you?

BETTY. I couldn't seem to. I – their man was beside me. All I could say was, 'Barney, Barney, wake up.' He asked me if his name was Barney. I didn't answer him, 'cause I didn't think it was any of his business. And then when we got – I saw this – I knew they were gonna want us to go on it. I didn't want to go. I kept telling them I'm not gonna go – I don't want to go. And he said for me to go ahead, go, that they just wanted to do some simple tests. As soon as they were over with, I'd go back to the car.

HYNEK. Did they tell you where they were from?

BETTY. No.

A wide variety of theories were put forward in explanation of the Hill case. It could be suggested, for example, that the abduction was a strong emotional reaction, a purely imaginary experience evoked by their anxiety at seeing the U.F.O. There was one notable feature in both Betty's and Barney's examination, which resembled a fertility test. A piece of apparatus was laid on Barney's genitals, while Betty was subjected to a painful examination with a needle passed through her navel.

Betty and Barney were both very popular at home and lived a highly social life. There was only one thing missing from it, and that was children. This might perhaps have provided the basis of an imaginary experience, in which the examination was a kind of compensation element.

Naturally there are many people who believe that everything happened exactly as the Hills described it. They argue that people can only tell the truth under hypnosis. And although practically everyone who had anything to do with the case confirmed that any kind of deception was more or less impossible, hypnosis cannot unfortunately be taken as absolute proof. Even under hypnosis, Betty and Barney Hill could only say what they believed to be true.

However that may be, there is one feature of the episode which is surprising, and that is the three-dimensional star map mentioned by Betty Hill. Her description sounds remarkably like holography (a form of laser photography which represents illuminated objects by reconstructing the light waves around them – the use of this process is still in its infancy on Earth). This star map was painstakingly reconstructed by the astronomer Marjorie Fish. (It will be remembered that people under hypnosis can remember the smallest details of experiences which have otherwise been forgotten.) Unfortunately none of it was identifiable as part of the night sky with which we are familiar.

Marjorie Fish gave her model to Dr Mitchell of Ohio State University, who subjected it to lengthy computer analysis and finally came to an amazing conclusion: Betty Hill's map shows a section of our Universe as it would appear from the star Theta Reticuli 1, thirty-six light-years away!

14

Close Encounters

After careful checking and analysis of the numerous U.F.O. sightings, experts were able to draw some conclusions about the phenomenon as early as the 1960s. In the modern U.F.O. era, certain patterns are clearly recognizable. During the Second World War, for example, the small, round 'foo fighters' appeared, to be replaced in the next stage, after the war, by compact, disc-shaped objects without any openings – i.e. windows or doors – and without any particular distinguishing features. The classic flying saucer with windows or a transparent dome did not appear until later. But throughout this whole period, large, cigar-shaped flying objects were also observed.

With the appearance of the saucers with viewing domes, reports began to come in from all over the world of so-called close encounters of the third kind.

If we try to analyse the different types of U.F.O. theoretically, the small foo fighters could possibly have been automatic observation probes, while the windowless and doorless disc-shaped objects could have been more complex, remote-controlled research probes. The classic U.F.O.s, with windows and viewing domes – assuming that these served for observation and vision by whatever beings were inside the saucers – would have represented manned spaceships.

The figures which appeared in the so-called close encounters all over the world seemed to share common features. Generally speaking the size of the U.F.O.s' occupants was described as being from three to four and a half feet. They had hairless heads which were described as being relatively large in comparison with their bodies. Typically, the mouth was described as a slit or opening, the nose inconspicuous, the eyes large and expressive and the complexion varying between white, ashen and clay-coloured. Most eyewitnesses spoke of markedly elongated limbs.

Naturally, allowances must be made for the eyewitnesses' differing powers of observation, which would probably be found to account for many of the differences of detail. We know from our experience of traffic accidents, for example, how ten different witnesses can produce different and often contradictory accounts of the same thing.

There is also the possibility, if we accept the existence of U.F.O.s, that they come from different worlds in different planetary systems, and this again could explain the differences in their appearance.

A number of experts have suggested that the U.F.O. phenomenon is a socio-psychological phenomenon, but if this is the case they must also explain why a North American Indian, a highly qualified French astronomer, a Russian pilot, an Australian sheep farmer, a German engineer and an Apollo astronaut seem to have had such conspicuously similar experiences with U.F.O.s. These experts would also have to explain how a so-called socio-psychological phenomenon can leave behind impressions of landing gear and other traces. Physical marks of this kind also seem to exclude the possibility that U.F.O.s are no more than holographic or psychic projections. The following episode speaks for itself.

One of the most fascinating U.F.O. sightings took place on 24 April 1964 in New Mexico. At 5.50 in the afternoon, thirty-one-year-old patrolman Lonnie Zamora from Socorro noticed a black Chevrolet passing southwards through the town, well above the speed limit.

At the same time a married couple driving with their three sons in a green Cadillac saw an egg-shaped flying object, apparently made of aluminium or magnesium, passing low over the highway. The driver was still cursing the reckless pilot when a white Pontiac patrol car sped past, and he commented to his family that it was obviously in pursuit of the 'flying road hog'.

The driver of the Cadillac stopped at the next petrol station to fill up and complained bitterly to the proprietor, Opal Grinder, and his son Jimmy about the pilot's behaviour, describing the strange aircraft to him.

In the meantime Zamora was in the southern quarter of the town, calmly waiting for his quarry in the black Chevrolet, who had disappeared into a cul-de-sac and must reappear at any moment. Suddenly he heard a roaring noise, and simultaneously saw a dazzling blue light, which seemed to come from an uninhabited area about 1,000 yards away on the other side of a gully.

Later, Zamora remembered that he saw dust rising and thought that something must have exploded in a dynamite store which was situated there. As a conscientious patrolman he naturally decided to investigate, and drove along the bumpy road to the crest of a hill from which he could survey the scene. About 700 yards away, down in the gully, he saw a white object which, from a distance, looked like a white car turned over on its side. Two small figures in white overalls were standing near the object, apparently inspecting it.

He called his headquarters on the radio and reported what he had seen, adding that he was going to drive over and take a closer look. He set out towards the gully, but lost sight of the object in a dip in the road. Finally he stopped thirty yards away from the object and got out. The machine was standing about twenty-five feet below him in the gully; it was now silent and the two figures had disappeared. Zamora said that the object was smooth, oval shaped and had no windows or doors. It was supported on what seemed to be landing gear.

Suddenly the object made a deafening noise. Zamora thought it was going to explode and ran back to shelter behind some bushes. Glancing over his shoulder, he saw that it was taking off vertically, and so he threw himself flat on the ground, covered his head with his arms and waited. When nothing happened, the patrolman risked a cautious glance towards the U.F.O. and was amazed to see that it was now hovering silently twenty-five feet above the ground. On its side he saw a red marking about twelve inches high, consisting of a half moon with a vertical arrow through it and a horizontal bar underneath. The U.F.O. remained where it was for a few seconds and then flew away along the gulley in a southerly direction.

Zamora sprang up and ran to his patrol car in order to inform his headquarters, but found he could not. His radio suddenly was not working, and it did not come on again until some time later. When it did, Zamora asked Sergeant Chavez of the State police to be sent to his aid.

Chavez reported that he found Zamora very distressed by what had happened. Chavez and Zamora went together into the gulley. A bush had been flattened, and six impressions were to be seen in the soft ground. Four of them were ten by eighteen inches in size and approximately rhomboid in shape. There were also two round impressions in the ground a few inches apart.

Chavez immediately informed the military who sent specialists, including Allen Hynek, to make further investigations.

Apart from the family in the Cadillac, two other witnesses had seen the egg-shaped flying object. They were Paul Kies and Larry Kratzer from Dubuque, Iowa, who were about two miles away from the gully, driving towards Socorro.

The secret services and the F.B.I. represented by J. Arthur

Byrnes Jr, naturally took charge of this case too. Zamora was urged not to say anything about it, particularly about the two white figures and the markings on the side of the alien machine.

'People would never believe you in any case,' were Byrnes's final words to Zamora.

When asked, Zamora, who was known as a sober and thoroughly reliable character, could only reply: 'I'd sure like to know what it was. But all I know is that I saw it. And that's that.'

The Air Force investigated the matter, but as in so many cases, was unable to explain the episode after the most searching investigations.

In 1965, forty-five-year-old farmer James Flynn was running a cattle ranch near Fort Myers, in Florida. He was highly regarded both among his neighbours and in the rest of the surrounding community, and considered a generally reliable person.

On 12 March he went out hunting in his buggy, taking his four dogs with him. He knew a remote spot in the Everglades, the marsh and swamp region of Florida, which lay about eleven miles south-east of the 'Big Cypress' Indian reservation. Both the journey and the first day of his stay there passed without incident. But on the next day, which was Sunday, the hounds scented a roebuck and gave chase. When Flynn whistled the dogs back, only one of them obeyed, and when the other three had not come back to camp by midnight, he decided to go in search of them, assuming that they had got lost. He drove after his last dog as it followed the scent of the roebuck, and around 1 o'clock in the morning noticed a gigantic gleaming light about a mile away among the cypresses. As Flynn watched, it flew three or four times above the trees, always returning to its point of departure.

Drawn by curiosity, Flynn now drove towards the light. Slowly, it seemed to move nearer to the ground, and as Flynn steered towards it through the lines of trees, it seemed to have almost landed. By this time, Flynn was no more than 450 yards away, and could see that it was not simply a light, but a gigantic, disc-shaped object. Looking through his binoculars, he found that it was a flying object shaped like a flattened cork and twice as broad as it was high. It was unmistakably made of metal and seemed to have four rows of windows running round it, the windows themselves being about two feet in diameter and each surrounded by a strip of black material. The bottom row was about thirteen feet above the underside of the object and the top row seemed to be about eight feet beneath the 'dome'. The U.F.O. was about seventy-two feet in diameter. Flynn arrived at these measurements by comparison with the cypress trees behind the object, whose height he already knew.

In describing the U.F.O. later, Flynn said that he had not noticed any insignia or markings on it. He saw nothing else apart from a dull yellow light through the windows and an orange glow from the underside of the object which lit up the ground beneath.

Now even more curious, Flynn started up his buggy and drove towards the strange object. A humming noise 'like the noise from a large transformer', as Flynn put it, got louder as he approached. Finally he got out and ran a couple of yards into the illuminated zone beneath the U.F.O., only to be swept out again immediately by a heavy blast of air. Flynn now waved up at the windows, without getting any reaction. After a minute he walked again. Now there was a reaction, in the form of a short, dazzling beam of light which was directed from one of the windows in the bottom row and hit him directly between his eyes. Flynn lost consciousness.

When he came to again, he was blind in his right eye, and the sight in his left eye was badly impaired. He crawled back to his buggy, where his dog, which had gone wild when he approached the object, was now lying, apparently indifferent to what had happened. As soon as his impaired vision allowed him,

Flynn searched the area, but could find nothing except for the tracks he had left when crawling away from the U.F.O.

A friendly Indian from the reservation eventually brought him back to Fort Myers. His wife took him straight to hospital for treatment, and it was only then that Flynn discovered that he had not been unconscious for two or three hours, but for a whole twenty-four.

The doctor who treated him, Dr Harvey Stipe, reported to A.P.R.O. in April 1965 that Flynn had suffered haemorrhages in the frontal eye region obviously of a traumatic nature. There was no evidence of paralysis but the deep reflexes of the tendons in the biceps, lower arm muscles, knee and tensor muscles, as well as the reflexes in the soles of the feet and stomach muscles did not respond. Only the reflexes on the inside of the thighs were functioning. In the course of five to eight days the reflexes began to function again, albeit irregularly.

After spending four days in hospital, Flynn began to recover from his deafness and the numbness in his arms and legs. But within twenty-four hours, the symptoms began again.

When Flynn was examined again on 16 April, four weeks after the episode, all his reflexes had returned to normal, except for those in the stomach, which had not entirely recovered. The dent over the eyes was still there and the acuity of vision in the right eye was still badly impaired. Dr Stipe, who had known Flynn for twenty-five years, wrote to the A.P.R.O. that he had always found him to be a highly reliable and psychologically stable person. He had also driven back to the site of the encounter with Flynn and at the place Flynn pointed out to him had found the tree-tops recently singed and burned in an exact circle – which he had photographed. Also, on two trees standing about five yards apart, the bark had been shaved off the trunk for about twenty inches in each case beneath the crown, as if some heavy object had scraped down it.

A few months after Flynn's adventure, a French lavender grower, Maurice Masse, from Valensole in the centre of the lavender-growing district in Alpes de Haute Provence, had an experience which was remarkably similar to that of Lonnie Zamora.

Masse was forty years old, father of two children and the owner of a lavender distillery in Valensole. During the month of July he had noticed with increasing annoyance that someone seemed to be stealing his young lavender plants. In the early morning of 1 July 1965, he was in the field which he called l'Olivol, hoeing the plants. It was 6 o'clock, and he was just about to start work again after stopping for a cigarette, when he noticed a whistling noise. He stood up from the heap of stones at the end of the small vineyard which ran alongside the field, and looked around, expecting to see a helicopter. But instead, he was amazed to see a strange-looking machine standing in the field some distance away. It looked like a rugby ball and was about as big as a Renault Dauphine. It stood on six legs about twenty inches above the ground and had something like a central axle.

Nearby, two figures were engaged in picking Maurice Masse's lavender plants. He watched angrily through the vines and finally ran towards the supposed thieves. One of them had his back to Masse, while the other was looking in his direction. When Masse was still ten yards away from the strangers, one of them suddenly turned and aimed a small object which he had in his right hand at Masse. He then put it in a holster on his left side. Masse was immediately paralysed; he could not move his head or limbs and had lost all feeling.

When Masse was later interrogated, he described the alien beings as small – perhaps four feet tall – but with a conspicuously large head which was joined almost without transition to the body. Masse stated that the aliens had had no hair, and a hole instead of a mouth. The eyes were like human eyes, but the lids had no lashes. They were smooth-skinned with complexions the colour of Central Europeans. Their shoulders were scarcely wider than their heads. The strangers had arms and legs, but Masse could not describe their hands and feet. They were wearing dark, skin-tight overalls, with a small container on the left side and a large one on the right.

Masse said that after a while they had climbed back into their machine, which was about eight feet high, and watched him through the transparent dome. A door like a roller blind closed upwards and the landing gear disappeared into the bottom of the machine. The U.F.O. then lifted off from the ground with a dull report and flew noiselessly away. After about thirty yards, it suddenly disappeared, as if a light had been turned out. Only the tracks it left on the field showed the direction it had taken.

It was not until fifteen minutes later that Masse was able to move again, and he went straight to the police to report the incident. At first he was questioned by two local policemen, Azias and Santoni. But on the next day, the investigation was taken over by Police Superintendent Valnet.

On investigating the sight where Masse claimed the machine had stood, he found the ground soft, although it had not been raining. There was also a circular depression with a diameter of four feet. In its centre was a hole sixteen inches deep and seven inches in diameter.

When Valnet asked him if he had been afraid, Masse replied in the negative, saying: 'The strangers had such a calm and peaceful aura about them that I was not in the least afraid.'

Masse too was stated by his colleagues, friends and neighbours to be absolutely trustworthy and of sound mind.

And in the place where Masse claimed that the U.F.O. landed, the lavender grew very poorly for many years to come.

While Maurice Masse was having his face-to-face encounter with a U.F.O. on his lavender field in France, scientists in the Antarctic were being confronted with a gigantic light in the sky, which put all the electrical and electronic apparatus in their research station out of action.

The episode took place at the Argentine research station on Deception Island in the Antarctic. It was here that a gigantic flying saucer was observed on 3 July 1965 at 10.40 local time, and recorded on colour film. The object was chiefly red or green, but its colour changed intermittently, ranging also through yellow, white, blue and orange. For twenty minutes, the gigantic object zigzagged overhead at an incredible speed and then hovered over the base at an altitude of 16,500 feet. The sky was cloudless, and lit by the moon in its last quarter, and throughout this period, scientists and staff of the research station watched the U.F.O. through binoculars.

The object caused strong electromagnetic disturbances in the electrical installations on Deception Island, interfering with instruments for measuring the Earth's magnetic field and radio transmitters and receivers.

The U.F.O. was observed again on the same day by Chilean scientists, at another base nearby, and also from an Argentine research station in the South Orkney Islands.

Detailed reports were made of these sightings, and confirmed by the Argentine Secretary of State for the Navy and the Chilean Minister for Communications.

In the years 1965 and 1966 a series of episodes occurred in which the C.I.A. found itself compelled to take an active interest; these occurrences so alarmed President Johnson that he ordered an immediate investigation.

In 1965, the astronauts James McDivitt and Ed White reported a silver object with antennae-like projections approaching their *Gemini IV* spacecraft during their twentieth orbit of the earth between Hawaii and the Caribbean. McDivitt was able to take a number of photographs, which were later closely analysed. The U.F.O. came nearer and nearer, and the two astronauts feared it would collide with them. But before they had done more than consider taking avoiding action, the object had disappeared without a trace. There were no satellites in the area during the encounter.

The astronauts Frank Borman and James E. Lovell also encountered a U.F.O. during their second earth orbit in *Gemini VII*, over Antigua. It slowed down and slowly drifted back past the astronauts' space capsule before disappearing from their sight.

Astronauts Young and Collins had a similar experience with two U.F.O.s which stationed themselves in front of their *Gemini X* space capsule and played 'pacemaker' with them for a while.

It need hardly be mentioned that astronauts are highly qualified technicians and observers, who by the very nature of their occupation are familiar with rockets and satellites, so that they are hardly likely to be mistaken.

Even more of a furore was caused when the Governor of Florida became involved in a U.F.O. sighting. On 25 April 1966, while conducting a campaign for his re-election, Haydon Burns was flying across Florida with his staff. There were eleven people in the party, including a number of journalists.

When the Governor cried, 'There's a U.F.O. out there,' everyone naturally rushed to the windows. Bill Mansfield, a reporter on the *Miami Herald*, whose article was to make national headlines the following day, saw a reflected orange glow, and thought a bush fire must have broken out, until he noticed that it was coming from two lights flying at about the same altitude as the Governor's aircraft and following it at about 250 m.p.h. Governor Burns was just coming out of the cockpit, where he had ordered the pilot to steer towards the strange lights, when these suddenly rose vertically and disappeared in an instant.

Naturally this spectacular sighting made headlines in the

American press, especially since Governor Burns – despite his election campaign – emphatically confirmed the U.F.O. sighting.

Further trouble was caused by a radar sighting of a U.F.O. on 27 August 1966 over a strategic missile base in North Dakota. Confronted simultaneously with the news of the sighting and the information that all communications with the outside world had been broken, the base commander panicked. And with good reason, since the base was equipped with a triple security system, designed to make any breakdown impossible. The U.F.O. shot vertically up into the sky at an incredible speed, the radar observers losing sight of it when it had reached an altitude of seventeen miles. At that moment, contact with the outside world was re-established.

Things had got to the point where the Air Force could no longer ignore the demands of the public and the President. They had to think of something, and they could no longer take refuge in the 'atmospheric' explanations of Dr Donald Menzel, which were being received with increasing incredulity by the public.

Menzel was an astrophysicist who had obtained his doctorate in 1924 and in later years had assumed the mantle of the high priest of ufology. In his standard work, *Flying Saucers*, he categorically attributed all U.F.O. phenomena, whether tracks in the sand or traces on a radar screen, to three basic causes:

1.   atmospheric disturbances,
2.   the planet Mars,
3.   the planet Venus.

(After Menzel's death, his doctrine was taken up by his friend, Philip Klass, the publisher of *Aviation Week*.)

Since Menzel's explanations were no longer being accepted, in particular by an increasing number of scientists, the C.I.A.

conceived a brilliant solution: they arranged for an 'independent' research project to be commissioned by the Air Force at the University of Colorado. The Air Force laid out the derisory sum of 300,000 dollars, which by the end of the project had grown to 500,000 dollars. Professor Edward U. Condon was appointed director of the project, and, with a few exceptions, his colleagues were experts from a wide variety of disciplines, including five without academic qualifications and a few students who had not yet completed their studies.

The end result of the project was a foregone conclusion. Condon, the 'independent scientist' had made his mind up before the investigation started, and never betrayed a shadow of doubt either in press interviews or on other occasions. His project coordinator and administrator, Robert J. Low, even went so far as to try to influence his colleagues in a memorandum. The background to this scandalous piece of jobbery only became known by chance. Low's memorandum, entitled 'Thoughts on the U.F.O. project', contained the following suggestion:

> The trick would be, I think, to describe the project so that, to the public, it would appear a totally objective study but, to the scientific community, would present the image of a group of nonbelievers trying their best to be objective but having an almost zero expectation of finding a saucer.

Before the start of the project, Condon had particularly recommended two experts, Drs Saunders and Levine. (They were later responsible for the publication of the Low memorandum.) But when they refused to share Condon's viewpoint and indeed expressed the opinion that U.F.O.s could be extra-terrestrial spaceships, Condon dismissed them for 'incompetence'.

Condon's administrative assistant in the project, Mary Louise Armstrong, handed in her notice pleading a lack of respect for Condon. Of the twelve permanent staff originally engaged for the project, Condon was eventually left with only two. All the others had left because of the constant intrigues and differences of opinion.

Although Dr David Saunders, now Professor of Psychology at the Universtiy of Colorado in Boulder, had prepared thousands of concrete U.F.O. cases for careful examination, the Condon report only dealt with ninety-one in all. Saunders, who today has one of the most comprehensive collections of data on U.F.O.s, stated that Condon's task had in fact been chiefly political in nature.

The closing report of the Colorado project was published in January 1969 as *Scientific Study of Unidentified Flying Objects*, commonly known as the 'Condon Report'. The paperback edition contains 965 pages, while the bound edition runs to 1485, and it concludes that there is no proof to justify the assumption that extraterrestrial visitors have penetrated the earth's atmosphere, and insufficient data to justify further research in this field.

Although the Colorado project deliberately investigated questionable sightings, in a few cases, paradoxically, it had to be admitted that they could not be explained. Of the ninety-one cases investigated, thirty had to be classified as genuine unidentified objects.

One example is the so-called McMinnville sighting in Oregon, which took place as follows.

At 7.30 one evening, the wife of farmer Paul Trent was feeding her rabbit in the garden when she saw a U.F.O. in the sky. She ran quickly into the house, called her husband, and at the same time fetched a camera. Paul Trent took two pictures, one while the object was moving in a north-westerly direction, and another as it tilted on its side and disappeared towards the west.

The Condon Report commented:

This is one of the few U.F.O. reports in which all factors

investigated, geometric, psychological, and physical, appear to be consistent with the assertion that an extraordinary flying object, silvery, metallic, disc-shaped, tens of metres in diameter, and evidently artificial, flew within sight of two witnesses.

If the Air Force and the C.I.A. believed that the Condon Report would let them off the hook, they were thoroughly mistaken, in fact, it merely intensified public criticism. There were rumours of intrigue and manipulation in the project's research methods. The Condon report as a whole had acquired the proportions of a scandal in the scientific world.

A study group from the American Institute for Aeronautics and Astronautics (A.I.A.A.), the largest space research organization in the world, investigated the Condon Report and came to some startling conclusions.

No less than thirty per cent of the U.F.O. cases which were investigated could not be explained. Condon's assertion that further investigation of U.F.O.s was completely useless clearly did not match the facts. Moreover his personal view that the Earth was unlikely to be visited by intelligent lifeforms from beyond our solar system in the next 10,000 years was scarcely a convincing reason for dismissing all further investigation as useless.

The panel of investigators came to the conclusion that even the rest of the well documented cases could hardly be ignored, since they represented the hard core of the U.F.O. controversy. This alone was grounds enough for further investigation and, contrary to Condon's assertion, there were considerable scientific advantages to be gained from it.

While the Condon project was causing a scandal in the United States, U.F.O. sightings in the U.S.S.R. were increasing to such an extent that the K.G.B. was unable to deal with them all by itself, and handed the investigation over to the scientists. On 18 October 1967, a U.F.O. research group was founded; it was given the name of the Permanent Cosmonautic Commission of the U.S.S.R., and its director was Major General of the Air Force Porfiri Stoljarov.

In contradistinction to the phoney Colorado Project, a thorough investigation was undertaken. Photographic, electronic and radar measuring methods were used in preference to others, and the group worked in conjunction with the Pulkovo Observatory and others throughout the Soviet Union. Important sightings were carefully investigated and analysed.

Among these was the sighting made by the passengers and crew of a TU-104, who on 23 September 1964 observed a disc-shaped, metallic object with a dome while flying between Moscow and Leningrad. The object was observed over Bologay, flying underneath the airliner and on a parallel course.

On 26 July 1965, R. Vitolmiek, the director of an ionospheric observation station in Ogra, Latvia, observed a flying disc about 300 feet in diameter through a telescope. It was accompanied by three smaller discs.

And on 8 August 1967 the astronomer Anatoli Sazanov of the Caucasian astrophysical observatory of Kislovodsk saw a disc-shaped object flying eastward at high speed across the northern sky. Ten of his colleagues were also present.

One sighting which was of particular interest for Stoljarov had taken place in space on 18 June 1963, when the cosmonaut Valery Bykovsky was followed by an egg-shaped object in his *Vostok VI* spacecraft. Bykovsky reported that it suddenly turned and shot away at an incredible speed. His description almost exactly matched that of the object sighted by Lonnie Zamora a year earlier in Socorro.

As was to be expected, the C.I.A. soon got wind of this Russian U.F.O. project and informed N.A.S.A. This in turn forced the Soviets to come out with their official explanation, and the Soviet Academy of Sciences duly reported that: 'Flying saucers don't exist.'

But behind locked doors, the Stoljarov committee was coming to very different conclusions. An interim report issued in 1970 stated that there were so many well documented sightings and radar traces as to rule out the possibility of optical illusions. They were clearly produced by concrete, real objects, the origin of which could only be explained by further, systematic research. It was therefore recommended that meteorological, astronomical, geophysical and hydrometeorological observation stations, and also satellites, should be commissioned to observe them. Moreover, the hypothesis that U.F.O.s are of extraterrestrial origin was the one which best fitted the data already collected.

15

Cross-Examination

The U.S. Air Force officially closed its U.F.O. project, Blue Book, on 17 December 1969. The case against it had been strengthened by the Condon Report, as well as by the criticism of Professor Allen Hynek, who is today director of the Lindheimer Astronomical Research Center at Northwestern University in Illinois. In a letter to Colonel Raymond S. Sleeper, commander of the Air Force's Foreign Technology Division, he condemned the general incompetence and unscientific approach of Project Blue Book, accusing it of having failed to investigate important cases in sufficient depth. But Hynek's major criticism was directed at the Air Force's pronouncement that U.F.O.s are not potentially dangerous; the fact that they had not so far been obviously hostile did not mean that this would also be the case in the future.

If the Air Force hoped that the abandoning of Project Blue Book would enable them to act like the proverbial three monkeys – hearing nothing, seeing nothing and saying nothing – the increasingly concrete reports of sightings which they were receiving must have been a disappointment to them.

On 14 September 1969, in fact, another sensational U.F.O. sighting was reported. This time it was from space. The *Apollo*

XII astronauts, P. Conrad, D. Gordon and E. Bean, the second team on the trip to the moon, reported that their space capsule was being accompanied by two U.F.O.s. In informing the control centre at Houston, Gordon described them as shining very brightly and apparently signalling to the capsule. He hoped they were friendly.

In view of this and similar occurrences, it is not surprising that the U.S. armed forces continue to take an unofficial interest in the U.F.O. phenomenon. There is, for example, a secret order to the American fleet connected with the early warning system for the defence of the North American continent, named Merint Report Procedure No. OPNAV 94-P-3B. It contains instructions for procedures in the case of attack by submarines and other warships; of air attacks by missiles and aircraft; or an alarm caused by *unidentified flying objects*. This secret order even contains a drawing of the typical saucer shape with a dome, and its prescriptions are still in force.

In April 1971 the influential *Industrial Research Magazine* published the result of a questionnaire about U.F.O.s. This journal has a readership of over 300,000 specialists in the fields of science and technology. The results of the questionnaire were published under the headline 'U.F.O.s probably do exist'. The survey had found that fifty-four per cent of all those questioned were convinced that U.F.O.s exist. Against this, thirty-one per cent denied their existence. By far the larger part of those questioned were of the opinion that information about U.F.O.s was being deliberately withheld, and eighty per cent believed that the Condon Report was not the last word on the subject. An astonishingly high proportion, thirty-two per cent, assumed that U.F.O.s were extraterrestrial spaceships; twenty-seven per cent, on the other hand, were convinced that they were natural phenomena. Six in a thousand suspected that experiments by the Eastern Bloc states were involved.

A year before this, engineers and scientists of the American Institute for Aeronautics and Astronautics had suggested that the only effective means of research lay in a sustained and vigorous effort towards more efficient and objective data collection and the use of highly sophisticated research methods. But, they said, such an approach to the problem would require not only an effort on the part of scientists and engineers, but also a readiness on the part of government departments to accept sensible proposals in this area of research, without being afraid of incurring criticism and ridicule.

On 13 June 1971 the highly qualified physicist Professor James McDonald of the Institute of Atmospheric Physics at Arizona University was found with a bullet in his head near the bridge over the Canyon del Oro in the Arizona desert.

Officially, it was a case of suicide – just as Jessup's death had been. But McDonald was a scientist of international standing, who was taken seriously by the U.N.

Like Jessup, McDonald had courageously tackled the U.F.O. problem. He had investigated U.F.O. sightings all over the world, and had not been afraid to put his reputation in the scientific establishment at risk. Like Jessup, he was convinced that the genuine U.F.O. sightings were of extraterrestrial spaceships observing and investigating the earth and its life forms. One sighting which interested McDonald in particular took place in Australia in the late autumn of 1967.

On 31 October of that year, an Australian sheep-farmer named Spargo was driving away from Konjonup at 9 o'clock in the evening. He had just paid his team of sheep-shearers there and was going on to Boyup Brook, where he had more people to pay.

He was driving along the little-used road under a clear, starlit sky, when his car suddenly stopped, for no apparent reason. The headlights were extinguished, the radio was silent, in fact the whole electrical system had suddenly become lifeless. Spargo could not understand it. He wondered why he had not been thrown through the windscreen when the car suddenly came to a halt. He had after all been travelling at 60 m.p.h.

And now he was stuck in the middle of nowhere without knowing why. The landscape was hilly, dotted with a few trees. All he was aware of was a brilliant beam of light shining right up into the sky, and he himself seemed to be caught in its focus.

Spargo eventually noticed that the light was coming from above, from a disc-shaped flying object which was hovering about 120 feet from the ground above the top of a tree. The U.F.O. could have been thirty feet in diameter, and the ray of light directed at Spargo seemed to come from a tube which projected from the floor of the U.F.O.

Then, just as suddenly as he had stopped, Spargo started to move again. But just as he could not remember having stopped the car, he did not know how he had started it.

Spargo now stopped deliberately, got out and looked up at the sky. He could see nothing but stars. Shaking his head he got in again and drove towards Boyup Brook. There he went straight to the police to report his strange encounter.

Spargo was later interviewed and thoroughly examined by a psychiatrist, Dr Paul Zeck. He told the doctor that he had felt 'shut in' by the tube. It had a diameter of about three feet and light shone from the outside of it. Inside there was nothing to be seen. Spargo had had the feeling that his car was lit up by the beam, but he couldn't or wouldn't turn round and so did not know if this was true. But he could not get rid of the feeling that he was being watched from this tube or through this tube. Spargo could make out nothing else apart from the outlines of the U.F.O.

He had felt an urge to look into the tube, but he had no idea why. He simply sat there and stared into it. Suddenly it went dark, like when someone turns the light out. The U.F.O.

changed shape, it became darker and suddenly flew away westwards at a fantastic speed. In a few seconds it was out of sight.

When Dr Zeck asked him about noises, Spargo could not remember having heard any sound at all. Spargo thought this very strange because normally in the bush at night, the frogs are croaking, the crickets are chirping and you can hear all kinds of noises.

The whole episode must have lasted five minutes, for on arriving in Boyup Brook, Spargo noticed that his watch, which was normally accurate to the second, was five minutes slow. It could only have stopped in the bush.

According to an article published in the *West Australian* of 1 November 1967, the U.F.O. had been observed by a number of farmers and sheep-farmers apart from Spargo.

Six years later, on 11 October 1973, a forty-five-year-old docker named Charles Hickson and his nineteen-year-old workmate Calvin Parker were sitting fishing after work on the pier of an abandoned wharf at Pascagoula, Mississippi. It was about 5.30 p.m. and dusk was falling, when the silence was unexpectedly broken by a whistling sound in the air, just like a whistling kettle, according to Hickson.

The two anglers watched, speechless, as two brilliant, pulsating lights sank slowly to the ground and appeared to land in the middle of a tip about fifteen yards away, amid automobile wrecks and other rubbish of all kinds.

Hickson and Parker stared incredulously at the strange flying object, which was about eight feet high and perhaps forty feet in diameter. As the U.F.O. landed the whistling noise ceased and the dazzling lights went out, leaving two openings or hatches. The object now opened, 'not exactly like a door', said Hickson later, and yellowish white light shone from inside. It now became clear that the object was not resting on the ground but hovering or standing a couple of feet above it. When three strange figures now appeared in the opening, the dockers began to feel uneasy. The beings stood there for a moment, then without warning floated across to the two men on the river bank and were on top of them before they knew what had happened. Two of them held Hickson by the arms, and at the same moment he felt himself being pricked. Parker was held by the third being. Hickson later reported that he had felt paralysed and could only move his eyes. At least he could now take a close look at the strange figures. They obviously had legs, but did not move them, and their feet were, in Hickson's words, similar to 'elephants' feet'. Their arms hung down at their sides with hands like claws.

Both men were very frightened. 'I was frightened enough myself,' said Hickson, 'but Parker was beside himself with fear.'

They were about five feet tall, but their heads were quite unlike a human head. It sat directly on the shoulders, without any neck at all. The 'skin' was wrinkled all over, with deep furrows stretching diagonally across the arms and face. Hickson described it as like elephant's skin though he thought it might have been just a covering. Where the mouth and eyes usually are, there were only slits, and there was only a suggestion of a nose. They could have been robots.

Parker had fainted the moment he was touched. Hickson however remained quite lucid throughout the three-quarters of an hour the episode lasted. He reported having felt weightless the moment he was touched. The figures transported him and Parker in a gliding or floating motion to the spaceship. Hickson said that he did not hear a sound, apart from a brief humming noise from one of the figures. Once inside the ship, he and Parker were separated.

In a room about ten feet square, Hickson was left lying, weightless, in the air. An 'optical eye' somehow came out of the wall and without any cable or fixing floated through space along his body. Two of the figures meanwhile turned him freely into a variety of different positions and poses, finally 'sitting him down' in the air at an angle of forty-five degrees with his feet pointing towards the ground.

After this they disappeared and Hickson was left alone for a while. When they came back, they took him and carried him back to the pier as they had fetched him.

There he saw Calvin Parker again for the first time. He was standing with his face towards the river and had stretched out his arms. He looked like a statue.

Hickson felt the aliens put him down, and his feet touched the ground, his sense of feeling returned, and his legs gave way, perhaps from fear.

He tried to crawl across to Parker, but before he reached him the whistling sound began again. When he looked round, the opening in the object was no longer to be seen, the blue lights were flashing as brightly as they had at first, and suddenly the object disappeared from view. Parker was in shock and Hickson had to slap his face a couple of times before he became aware of his surroundings again. He had completely lost his grip, but finally Hickson was able to speak to him again, and assure him that the spaceship had really gone.

At first the two dockers agreed to keep their experience to themselves, since they were convinced that no one would believe them. But in the end they telephoned the sheriff of Pascagoula. They could only talk to his deputy, Captain Ryder, who at first believed the two dockers were trying to play a joke on him. But something in Parker's voice made him listen, and he told the two men to come to the police station.

No sooner were the two men through the station house door than they asked to be given a lie-detector test. Parker was still in a state of shock.

Sheriff Diamond and Captain Ryder interrogated the two men separately for many hours, and finally put them in a room which was bugged. When the police officials had listened to the tape-recordings of their conversation, they had not the slightest doubt that the dockers had told the truth. Although grilled repeatedly, they never once contradicted themselves. Both men were interrogated by experts from a wide variety of disciplines, including Professor James A. Harder, a specialist in hypnosis from the University of California. Harder hypnotized both of them, and came to the conclusion that the two men had described a real experience. Even with lie-detector tests their stories could not be faulted. In personality assessments, psychologists rated Hickson and Parker as balanced, simple, honest, intelligent, although without a high level of education.

On 5 November 1975, a group of tree-fellers eleven miles south of Heber in Arizona had finished their day's work and were on their way home. It was already dusk, and they were driving down a forest track when they saw something shining through a clump of trees. At first they thought it must be the last rays of the sun shining over a hilltop. But when they came round the obstruction they saw a U.F.O. hovering in a clearing. The men all started shouting together and the twenty-eight-year-old driver, Mike Rogers, stopped the truck.

The object was disc-shaped, and about twenty-five feet in diameter. It was floating about sixteen feet above the ground, was perhaps ten yards away from the truck and spread a warm light which bathed the whole area in a golden glow.

One of the tree-fellers, Travis Walton, jumped down from the truck and ran towards the U.F.O. His workmates were horrified and shouted out: 'Come back, you're crazy!'

But Walton did not hear, and crawled nearer through the undergrowth, until he heard a shrill noise and stood up. At the same moment he lost consciousness. A dazzling beam of light had issued from the object and hit him in the chest.

The driver shouted: 'Quick, shut the door!' and drove off at top speed. Once at a safe distance he stopped, and the men watched as the brilliant glow between the trees suddenly went out again. The tree-fellers now drove back to the place where the U.F.O. had stood and looked for Walton, but he had disappeared without a trace.

Five days later he reappeared, completely exhausted, and with the marks of injections on his arm. He claimed that he had been set down again on the road about six miles from the place where the U.F.O. had appeared.

As Walton was unable to remember his experience in detail, he was questioned about the episode under hypnosis in the presence of a number of doctors, including Howard Kandell, Joseph Saltz, Jean Rosenbaum and Robert Gamelin. After a session lasting eight hours, it transpired that he had woken from the unconsciousness produced by the ray of light to find himself lying on a metal table, with severe pains in his head and chest. He had thought he was in a hospital. Three figures about five feet high were bending over him. They had narrow faces, bald heads and large, brown, oval eyes. Their skin was chalky white and their hands had five fingers without nails.

Walton could not say how long the investigation lasted, because although he thought himself to be conscious, he also thought he was in a deep sleep. When he woke he found himself on the road near the place where he had first seen the U.F.O. After their investigation, the team of doctors came to the conclusion that Walton must have told the truth when he said that he had been in a U.F.O.

Walton's five workmates – Dwayne Smith, Alan Dalis, Kenneth Peterson, Mike Rogers and John Goulette – confirmed that Walton had run towards the U.F.O. Then a dazzling blue light had emerged from the object and hit him in the middle of the chest. He must have received something like a high-voltage electric shock, since he flew several yards through the air. The last thing they saw of him was his silhouette. Then he was gone, simply disappeared.

The exobiologist Carl Sagan maintains that it is mathematically as impossible for U.F.O.s to be visitors from outer space as it is for Father Christmas to visit every home within a space of eight hours on Christmas Eve – even if Father Christmas could travel faster than light, which science considers impossible.

More specifically, Sagan argues against the idea that U.F.O.s are extraterrestrial spaceships as follows:

> Let us presuppose the existence of a million stars with their attendant planets and highly developed civilizations. Let us also presuppose that the life-span of such a civilization under favourable conditions would be 10 million years. If each of these civilizations sent out just one ship to explore space per year, and each of these made only one contact, this would mean a million spaceships arriving somewhere or other each year. In the Milky Way there are at least 10,000 million planets which would be worth a visit. Thus in order for a single spaceship to visit the earth each year, each civilization would have to send out 10,000 spaceships. That would mean 10 million spaceships leaving their home planets in the Milky Way every year.

Sagan considers this totally impossible. For even if there were a civilization sufficiently in advance of our own, the idea that it would be able to send out 10,000 spaceships a year, only one of which would reach the earth, seems quite out of the question.

But here Sagan seems to be lacking his normal clear-sightedness and intelligence. In the first place it can be argued that a civilization which had reached the stage of space travel would start by exploring its near surroundings, which in astronomical terms would mean stars within a distance of perhaps twenty light-years. The number of spaceships required for this would be relatively small. Second, such a civilization, if it were envisaging sending out expeditions, would undoubtedly search the area systematically first, by listening in to radio signals and communications, for example, or through the spectral analysis of stars. And once it had successfully located an inhabited world it would most probably return to it again and again.

Paradoxically, Sagan accepts the possibility that the earth might have been visited by astronauts from outer space many thousands of years ago. So why should the same thing not happen today?

On 18 September 1976 at around 10.30 p.m., anxious inhabitants on the outskirts of the Iranian capital, Tehran, telephoned the control tower of the airport to report an unusual apparition in the night sky.

The airport staff were unable to make out anything themselves, but they nevertheless informed the Air Force base at Shahrokhi. Here the announcement was no longer news. The radar screens had long since picked up an unidentified flying object about eighty miles north of Tehran. It was shining so brightly that it could even be seen with the naked eye.

Two F-4 Phantoms were sent up to intercept the U.F.O., but as soon as they approached it all their communications systems were suddenly blocked, and the electronics, including the navigation system and firing control system ceased to function. Bewildered, the Phantom pilots turned back towards their base – and at the same moment everything began functioning again.

In the meantime the information came from the control tower that the object was moving slowly in a north-westerly direction, and the interceptors were ordered to follow them. According to radar measurements, the U.F.O. seemed to be the same size as a Boeing 707. Observers using binoculars could make out green, red, orange and blue lights.

Suddenly, a smaller object shot out of the U.F.O. towards the Phantoms. One of the pilots panicked, fearing that there was going to be a collision, and fired an AIM-9 rocket at the object. Immediately, all the electronic systems failed again. The pilot quickly steered away from Tehran towards the desert, while his companion in the other machine climbed into the sky and watched as the small disc-shaped object returned to the larger U.F.O. with the lights.

The Phantoms never had a chance of getting close to the U.F.O., since as soon as they got nearer than a certain distance, their instruments ceased to function. Finally they had to return to base for lack of fuel.

If, following Sagan's hypothesis, the U.F.O. which appeared over Tehran was not an extraterrestrial spaceship, any more than it was Father Christmas, what could it have been?

In fact, U.F.O.s – assuming that they are extraterrestrial spaceships – would not even have to exceed the speed of light in order to travel from one star to another.

And this is due to some rather startling consequences of Einstein's special theory of relativity.

The crew of a spaceship moving at near light speed is subject to so-called time dilatation. Because of this, everything runs more slowly for the space traveller – not only his clocks, but his heartbeat, his metabolism and the rate of decay of the atoms in his body and of those in the spaceship itself. As a result he ages far more slowly than his contemporaries who have stayed at home.

Time dilatation is tantamount to a journey into the future. The crew of a spaceship travelling at near light speed could travel right across the Milky Way *in less than the lifetime of one man.* But on returning to their home planet, they would land *approximately 200,000 years in the future.*

It is possible of course that a highly developed civilization could invent some process which would neutralize this difference of time on the return journey. In fact as a result of the special theory of relativity, it would even be possible to travel across the entire universe within the lifetime of one man, and in this case, the time dilatation would be so great that *even the solar system of the travellers would have ceased to exist.*

We cannot imagine the technology which would be needed to construct a spaceship capable of accelerating to near light speed. So it is idle to speculate how U.F.O.s are driven – whether by anti-gravity, electromagnetic energy, anti-matter-photon drive or some other system beyond our comprehension. As Sagan so rightly says:

> Civilizations hundreds or thousands of millions of years beyond us should have sciences and technologies so far beyond our present capabilities as to be indistinguishable from magic. It is not that what they can do violates the laws of physics; it is that we will not understand how they are able to use the laws of physics to do what they do.

On 20 September 1977 at around 4 o'clock in the afternoon, a gigantic disc appeared over the Soviet town of Petrozavodsk on the western shore of Lake Onega. It was 'as big as a football field', in the words of the inhabitants, many of whom witnessed the alarming phenomenon.

T.A.S.S. correspondent Nikolai Milov questioned hundreds of the inhabitants of Petrozavodsk, who reported that the U.F.O. had directed five intense beams of light on to the town, and that they had remained bathed in this light throughout the twelve minutes that the object had remained overhead.

Holes were found burned into window-panes and paving stones. Government officials took possession of panes with holes of different sizes, which were taken to research laboratories for examination. Many of the inhabitants were hysterical with fear and shouted, 'It's the end!', believing that the U.F.O. was an American nuclear weapon which would explode at any moment.

Among the eyewitnesses was the director of the Petrozavodsk meteorological station, Yuri Gromov, who reported that a small U.F.O. had detached itself from the large object, whereupon both of them had disappeared through the clouds. The internationally known Soviet geophysicist Alexei Zolotov commented: 'In my opinion it was a typical U.F.O.'

For the time being, then, we must conclude that the U.F.O. phenomenon is not a question of knowledge, but of experience. While experience cannot be effectively communicated, knowledge can.

For those who have actually encountered a U.F.O., this experience is reality. Sceptics to whom this experience must be communicated naturally remain sceptics. But for the time being, there is only experience, to which knowledge must take second place. But we can surely hope that sooner or later knowledge and experience will coincide.

High-Level Attitudes

What do the world's politicians and scientists and the populations of different countries think of the question of whether there are visitors from outer space? While in some European countries the idea tends to be summarily dismissed as 'primitive superstition' or 'foolish nonsense', more than half of all Americans believe in the U.F.O. phenomenon. More than 15 per cent of the American population have participated in opinion polls after U.F.O. sightings. Even Jimmy Carter believes in U.F.O.s, because he has seen one himself.

European governments tend to avoid pronouncing on U.F.O.s as far as possible, being content to allow the United States and Russia a monopoly of large-scale U.F.O. research. It is nevertheless significant that the question of U.F.O.s was recently debated in Britain's House of Lords.

The fact that Jimmy Carter has himself seen a U.F.O. has perhaps strengthened the general impression that ufology is a speciality of the United States.

In 1973, three years before he became President, Carter claimed that he and twenty others had seen a U.F.O. after he had made a speech to the Lyons Club in Thomaston in his home state of Georgia. The object was very bright, kept changing colour, and was about as big as the Moon. Carter and his companions watched it for ten minutes, but none of them could make out what it was. The experience convinced him that there are indeed unidentified objects in the sky.

During Carter's campaign for the presidency, his twenty-five-year-old son Jeff gave more details about the former Governor of Georgia's strange experience. It seems that the U.F.O. had three lights, which together were as big as the Moon. Its colour changed from red to green and it was situated near the Moon. He and others point out that Carter had served in the Navy and was a specialist in nuclear technology. He knows what natural phenomena in the sky look like and what aircraft look like.

Jimmy Carter's seventy-nine-year-old mother Lillian also remembered the episode. 'The U.F.O. made a mighty strong impression on Jimmy – he's told me about it several times. He's always been a serious boy, with both feet on the ground. And what he saw – as far as I can judge – is as sure as money in the bank.'

Shortly after his experience, Jimmy Carter announced that if he got into the White House, he would make sure that all the information there is in the U.S.A. about U.F.O. sightings would be made accessible to the public and scientists.

Commenting on Jimmy Carter's announcement, Jack Acuff, of the National Investigations Committee on Aerial Phenomena said in Washington that if a president of the United States ever released the hitherto unpublished material on U.F.O.s which is lying locked up in the national archives, it would be a sensation for the scientific world and also of immense value to the community. Acuff thought it was of the greatest importance that a personality like Carter had made such a pronouncement.

In the meantime Jimmy Carter has been President of the United States for over two years. But people throughout the world are still waiting for him to keep his promise.

He has in fact ordered N.A.S.A. to start new investigations into sightings of flying saucers, but the secret archives have yet to be opened to the American public.

In an interview, Frank Press, who advises President Carter in scientific questions, reported a renewed interest in unidentified flying objects. His office is receiving an increasing number of enquiries from the public, but is not in a position to answer them all. He suggested that the American space authority, N.A.S.A., should become active again in this field.

In response to this proposal, N.A.S.A. officials objected that U.F.O. research is extremely expensive, and suggested that a committee should first of all be appointed to discover whether such a measure was justified. Dave Williamson, who is responsible for N.A.S.A. special projects, is still opposed to the idea. He wants concrete evidence before he takes U.F.O. research any further.

'What we need,' he says, 'is a little green man, or a piece of metal from a U.F.O., which we can go to work on.'

Without this kind of proof, U.F.O. research remains in much the same dilemma as the search for the Loch Ness monster.

We can scarcely hope for little green men, but metal fragments which supposedly came from a U.F.O. do exist. In 1967, small metal fragments which had come from exploded U.F.O.s were found on the Brazilian coast near Ubaitaba and in the American state of South Dakota. The explosion of these objects had been observed by a whole series of witnesses. The fragments discovered after the explosions were minutely analysed in the United States by the Dow Chemical Company, the Oak Ridge atomic research centre in Tennessee and the University of Colorado. They were proved unequivocally to be made of ultra-pure magnesium, according to the July 1968 issue of *Industrial Research Magazine*. Magnesium, strong but light, would be a good material to meet the structural requirements of a flying saucer.

Since that time the U.F.O. research centre at Evanston in the

U.S.A. has received new films of U.F.O.s for evaluation, which were shot in Mexico, Guatemala and the Bahamas.

In France numerous supposed U.F.O.s have been sighted on radar screens. The French Ministry of Defence issued a denial when asked whether Mirage fighters had pursued U.F.O.s over France, but there can be no doubt that the national defence authorities were seriously involved in the question of unidentified flying objects.

The former French Minister for the Army, Robert Galley, declared in an interview: 'Sightings have been made by pilots, and our police force also reports on occurrences of this kind. However, the French Air Force has come to the conclusion that U.F.O.s do not represent any military danger.'

The phenomena have been investigated by the Centre National d'Études Spaciales (National Space Research Centre), whose work is of great importance for the whole nation.

For years the United Nations has been criticized for failing to solve the problems of our own planet. Now it looks as though it will also have to deal with the problems presented by other worlds. The U.N. agreed in general assembly to place the proposal of the former Prime Minister of Grenada, Sir Eric Gairy, for the 'recognition of extraterrestrial intruders', on the agenda. This means that in its next session the U.N. will debate the proposal to set up a U.N. committee for carrying out and co-ordinating U.F.O. research.

Gairy said that it was important to set up orderly contacts between the Earth and beings from other solar systems. The United Nations, he suggested, was the appropriate body to do this. More than 120 U.N. member states were present when the Grenadan Prime Minister reproached the governments of individual countries with drawing a thick veil of secrecy over 'these alarming episodes'. The time had come, he said, for a change.

At present, however, the U.N.'s Secretary-General, Kurt

Waldheim, is proving as tardy in taking measures as President Carter.

The director of the 'International U.F.O. Report Centre', Dr D. William Hauck reported: 'Shortly after the failure of Kurt Waldheim's attempt to become Austrian President, I asked him whether the authorities in his country would suppress U.F.O. reports. He replied that the Austrian government would publish any important information as soon as it was informed of it.'

After Kurt Waldheim became Secretary-General of the United Nations, there was some hope of paving the way to a common international attempt at solving the U.F.O. problem. In order to achieve this it would naturally be necessary for the different nations to pool their knowledge, in order to convince the member states of the phenomenon's international importance.

'I would willingly work under the auspices of the U.N. with anyone who is interested in fighting the official policy of secrecy,' says Dr Hauck.

Since the Western nations are not particularly forthcoming, it may be asked if the Eastern bloc is any more so. Are there any official pronouncements from the Communist camp?

I do not know of any official statements from the governments or from the Communist parties – which amounts to the same thing – behind the Iron Curtain. But scientists from these countries have expressed themselves with notable frankness.

Dr Felix Zigel of the Institute of Aeronautics in Moscow, for example, has said: 'There are reliably substantiated reports of U.F.O. sightings from the U.S.S.R. It can hardly be assumed that they are all merely optical illusions. For optical illusions can hardly show up on film, nor are they registered by radar. Thus the most convincing hypothesis is that U.F.O.s are vehicles from extraterrestrial civilizations.'

Professor V. F. Kuprevich, the President of the Soviet Academy of Sciences, came to a similar conclusion: 'Who knows – perhaps these beings from other planets are already visiting our earth – but do not want to make contact with us. Why? I should imagine it is because these intelligences are far beyond our present state of development, and to them we seem like the first cavemen.'

The Soviet rocket expert, Professor Ananoff has said: 'I am not disinclined to believe in flying saucers. It would hardly be surprising if there were other beings in the Universe besides us.'

Professor Vladarov stated that the Moscow Academy for Space Research had come to the conclusion that U.F.O.s could not be any form of sensory illusion, i.e. natural phenomena which could be explained in astronomical, geological or meteorological terms. Rather, they were flying machines of a variety of different forms, which must be made of some un-known, concrete material.

To Western eyes, the Soviet Union is engaged in intensive U.F.O. research, although the Soviet Academy of Sciences labelled this 'unscientific' in 1978. But in view of the amount of Soviet research being undertaken in the field of 'unscientific, parapsychological phenomena', this official declaration must be assumed to be politically motivated. In reality the All Soviet Cosmonautic Committee is a secret U.F.O. study group, which works together with the Soviet Air Force. There are also a number of scientists engaged in private U.F.O. research, notably Dr Modest Agrest and Dr Felix Zigel.

The People's Republic of China even uses its gigantic radio network to report U.F.O. sightings by means of simple code signals. The Americans have picked up numerous short-code signals from the Chinese mainland, and the Chinese keep a particularly close watch on their airspace.

In America it has almost become a tradition for politicians, and especially the President, to involve themselves in the U.F.O. phenomenon – though it is obviously a world-wide problem and not an exclusively American one. Back in November 1954, President Dwight D. Eisenhower said: 'I doubt the assumption that flying saucers only originate from one planet.'

The late John F. Kennedy went even a step further: 'I am convinced that spaceships come from other worlds than our own,' he said in February 1961.

His brother Robert, who was also assassinated, put his opinion in writing:

> I follow all reports on unidentified flying objects with the greatest interest and hope that we will one day discover more about them. I would be in favour of further research in this area in the hope that we can clarify the real facts about flying saucers.

John F. Kennedy's successor, President Johnson, was officially involved in the U.F.O. phenomenon when he was still a senator. In July 1960 he answered a written enquiry as follows:

> I have forwarded your interesting U.F.O. material to the staff of the P.I.S. As you may know, I have ordered that the latest developments in this field should be followed up closely and I am kept constantly informed of all significant U.F.O. sightings.

Nelson Rockefeller, former Vice-President of the United States, said when he was Governor of the State of New York that the American people should be suitably informed about every matter of national importance, so it is vitally necessary for American democracy that the general public should be informed about U.F.O.s too, immediately and unhesitatingly.

And Barry Goldwater, ex-presidential candidate and Air Force General in the Reserve, has said that he is convinced that Earth has been visited more than once by extraterrestrial intelligences. He said that naval and airline pilots had informed him of cases in which U.F.O.s came to within a few yards, only to fly away again at incredible speed. Although he had never seen a U.F.O. himself, he believed the reports of others.

This belief was attacked by *Der Spiegel* on 24 April 1978 in a highly critical article entitled 'The U.F.O.s are coming', part of which ran as follows:

But at present superstition is flourishing with almost medieval vigour.

With an enthusiasm which could hardly have been envisaged a decade ago, men in the Western industrial states – including intellectuals – have turned away from their once high expectations of science: people disappointed in the scientific age who have rediscovered Hermann Hesse's mysticism or turned to Zen Buddhism or transcendental meditation.

The decline into irrationality as a mass phenomenon is evident both from the best-seller lists and from the growing enthusiasm for mystical groupings and the newly awakened U.F.O. cult.

In fact *Der Spiegel* is wrong in classing this 'superstition' and 'decline into irrationality' as a purely Western phenomenon. In 1968 the *Soviet Weekly* said:

It can safely be asserted that the U.F.O. problem has taken on a global character and thus also requires global methods of investigation . . .

International scientific cooperation towards the solution of this problem would have long since been possible had it not been hindered by sensation-seeking and irresponsible, unscientific statements about flying saucers . . .

Regrettably, certain scientists in both East and West – in the Soviet Union and the U.S.A. – have chosen to dispute the very existence of this problem, instead of contributing to its solution.

It is by no means impossible that this solution would lead to a radical change in our thinking processes.

U.N. representatives from many different countries had already expressed their anxiety about U.F.O.s to the Secretary-General of the U.N., U Thant, in 1967. Thus U Thant knew that this phenomenon is by no means a special problem of Western industrial states, but is in fact a global phenomenon. It was not for nothing that he told U.N. representatives: 'Next to the Vietnam War, U.F.O.s are the most important problem confronting the United Nations.'

In a letter to U Thant, dated 5 June 1967, the late Dr James E. McDonald, Professor in the Department of Meteorology in the Institute of Atmospheric Physics at the University of Arizona, requested that the United Nations should take immediate measures to clarify the U.F.O. phenomenon:

I wish to thank you again for making it possible for me to meet with the United Nations Outer Space Affairs Group on 7 June, to discuss international scientific aspects of the problem of unidentified flying objects.

Enclosed is a copy of the statement which I am submitting, on 7 June, to the Outer Space Affairs Group. It summarizes briefly my reasons for urging immediate United Nations action on the U.F.O. problem. The problem is one of very large dimensions, so a brief summary of this sort can only present in barest outline the apparent nature of the U.F.O. problem and possible modes of scientific attack. I believe that a serious and determined effort on the part of the United Nations to assemble information on the problem and to encourage immediate scientific attention to the problem among all member nations would be a substantial step towards removing the 'ridicule lid' that is now so powerfully suppressing public reporting of many U.F.O. sightings. Many other U.N. actions could and should be taken to escalate world scientific concern for the U.F.O. problem.

As I have indicated in my enclosed statement to the Outer Space Affairs Group, I believe that very serious consideration must be given to the hypothesis that these unconventional objects constitute some form of extraterrestrial probes. Until I undertook personal study of the problem I was not able to give credence to such a hypothesis. After a year's intensive study I must still regard it as only a hypothesis, but I must emphasize that my findings drive me strongly toward the view that this may be the only presently acceptable hypothesis to account for the quite astonishing number of credibly reported low-level, close-range sightings of machine-like objects that are now on record from all over the world.

I wish to offer whatever personal assistance or counsel you or your colleagues might be able to draw from my own experience in studying this problem. The U.F.O. problem is an eminently international scientific problem. The United Nations, has, I believe, both responsibilities and obligations to accelerate serious scientific study of the U.F.O. problem throughout the world. To many serious students of the U.F.O. phenomena, it appears conceivable that something in the nature of a global surveillance by U.F.O.s has been underway in recent years. If there is even a remote chance that this view is correct, then our present ignorance of the purpose and plan of such surveillance must be speedily replaced by maximal understanding of what is going on. If the entire phenomenon is of some other nature, we need to know this. Present ignorance, present neglect, present ridicule all constitute regrettable features of our collective attitudes towards what may be a matter of urgent importance to all the peoples of the world.

United Nations scrutiny of the matter is, in my opinion, urgently needed.

The astrophysicist and computer scientist, Dr Jacques Vallée, who lived in America and worked for four years with Allen Hynek, writes in his book *The Invisible College*:

1. The things we call unidentified flying objects are neither objects nor flying. They can dematerialize, as some recent photographs show, and they violate the laws of motion as we know them.

2. U.F.O.s have been seen throughout history and have consistently received (or provided) their own explanation within the framework of each culture. In antiquity their occupants were regarded as gods; in medieval times, as magicians; in the nineteenth century, as scientific geniuses. And finally, in our own time, as interplanetary travellers. (Statements made by occupants of the 1897 airship included such declarations as, 'We are from Kansas' and even 'We are from ANYWHERE . . . but we'll be in Cuba tomorrow.')

3. U.F.O. reports are not necessarily caused by visits from space travellers. The phenomenon could be a manifestation of a much more complex technology. If time and space are not as simple in structure as physicists have assumed until now, then the question, 'Where do they come from?', may be meaningless; they could come from a place in *time*. If consciousness can be manifested outside the body, then the range of hypotheses can be even wider.

'Why are the scientists keeping quiet?' asks Vallée. 'Many astronomers must know the same as I do from my time at the Paris Observatory, namely that we had traced unidentified objects and even photographed them. There were films too.'

In a résumé of the situation, Vallée says:

In a few European states the American U.F.O. project was followed with strong interest. The British displayed no more than quiet restraint but in France the American decision was regarded with tense expectation: it was official French policy to represent the position of the U.S.A. in this matter. There was some explosive material in the European documents. Many sightings were remarkably well documented, and investigations at the highest level were carried out much more carefully and professionally than had been the case with the best incidents in the documents in the files of the U.S. Air Force. This was not surprising, for some of the eyewitnesses were high-ranking politicians. In one Western European state a near landing had taken place on the private estate of a head of state. The vehicle had been described in all details by members of the personal staff of this politician. This meant that the case had not been suppressed by the local police authorities; nor even by trustworthy scientists; the investigations were carried out by secret service specialists at high level.

According to one of the reports on this occurrence, the chauffeur of this head of state was driving through the private estate when he saw something about to land on the road ahead of him, which he took to be an aeroplane. He immediately braked to a halt. The object passed a few feet above the car, causing a violent vertical vibration. A few seconds later the object came back in the opposite direction, causing the same effect on the car as before. It then returned to the position over the trees where it had first appeared, abruptly changed altitude, banking through ninety degrees, and shot away towards the west.

The report continued:

The witness is absolutely reliable. We have found out that the object looked like an inverted soup-plate, with a central cockpit and *portholes*, and had a diameter of about sixty-five feet. An observation of this kind is no joke. Neither the U.S. Air Force nor the American academic establishment could have any idea of the extent of the problem in Western Europe. But the Russians were probably even more interested in it than the Western Europeans.

Unfortunately we are given no data on name, place and date for this sensational European sighting – assuming that it is genuine. This is all the more regrettable as Vallée is internationally considered the best informed expert in the U.F.O. field, and could therefore be expected to provide such information.

Vallée's statement that 'U.F.O.s are neither objects nor flying. They can dematerialize' is not altogether comprehensible. Admittedly, in many of the reported U.F.O. sightings, the object seems to disappear on the spot. The so-called 'hard' sightings (when a 'hard', i.e. metallic, object can be clearly seen) would in this case be temporary materializations in the earthly atmosphere; and so-called 'soft' sightings would be those in which the object appears as a blurred light form – a phase of materialization. In this case U.F.O.s would not match our concept of a spaceship as fabricated machines, which retain their material and mechanical structure on interstellar journeys.

But they would nevertheless be flying objects as soon as they were flying through the planetary atmosphere. And in most reports they do in fact behave like flying objects.

In fact it seems unlikely that a spaceship could retain its material structure on interstellar journeys, when we consider the gigantic differences in time and space between the different solar systems. Interstellar journeys are only possible if there are spaceships capable of travelling at something approaching the speed of light. At present there is no form of propulsive energy – at least on Earth – which would make this possible.

Spaceships which travel from star to star obviously embody scientific knowledge which we can scarcely dream of, and such revolutionary knowledge would no doubt enable them to take short cuts through other space-time dimensions. Dematerialization of the spaceship would most probably be a precondition for this. The appearance and behaviour of unidentified flying objects would be consistent with such a procedure.

What in fact are U.F.O.s? Opinions are still strongly divided. For example, the New York psychoanalyst, Dr Ernest H. Taves, says:

We are surrounded by U.F.O.s day and night, apparitions in the sky which are only waiting to be discovered. The observer sees them and often correctly identifies them as what they are: planets, reflected starlight, aerial reflections, meteorological-optical effects, Northern Lights, meteorites, aircraft, balloons, shiny pieces of paper carried high by the wind, flying bundles of prairie hay, ball lightning, St Elmo's fire, clouds, the Moon seen through mist, burning oil-wells, satellites re-entering the atmosphere, parachutes, missiles on test, reflections of headlights, birds, swarms of insects, kites, vapour trails, small airships, bubbles, glow-worms, optical illusions, dandelion heads, clouds of dust, etc., etc... The U.F.O. field is becoming the private domain of lunatics and religious fanatics.

Thus Taves. Today the church is still silent on the subject. Only the director of the Zentralstelle für Weltanschauungsfragen (Central Bureau for Questions of World Belief) in Stuttgart, Dr Hutten, was able to confirm to me an earlier statement in which he said: 'The history of the spirit has become richer by the so-called science of ufology. It is a Cosmic parallel to spiritualism.'

In his view the wave of interest in U.F.O.s which began in the United States, is one of the 'multifarious and extensive protest movements which has been set off by secularism.'

'Some time or other,' says Dr Hutten, 'Ufology will become a message of salvation with a Christian stamp to it.'

According to his theory, a 'Cosmic Advent' will come through the combination of the planetary host with the inhabitants of the Earth. If men take the advice of these planetary beings, and in particular cease testing atomic bombs, then they will be able to join the 'great Cosmic federation', which will ensure Cosmic trade and a future without war, poverty and suffering.

'If there have been so many hundreds of U.F.O. landings – as some believers maintain – why haven't they left the slightest trace of their presence, except for evidence which any schoolboy could have fabricated?' says Philip J. Klass, editor in chief of the American magazine *Aviation Week and Space Technology*.

R. Leo Sprinkle, Professor of Psychology at the University of Wyoming, has this to say on the subject of the existence of U.F.O.s: 'Your question reminds me of the story of the Irishwoman who was asked if she believed in fairies. "No," she replied, "but they're there." It's the same with U.F.O.s. Whatever they are, they're definitely there.'

Bibliography

'.A.I.A.A. committee looks at the U.F.O. problem', *Astronautics and Aeronautics*, December 1968.

Bourret, Jean-Claude. *U.F.O.: Spekulationen und Tatsachen: Eine Dokumentation*. Tübingen: Edition Sven Erik Bergh, 1977.

Bowen, Charles (ed.). *The Humanoids*. London: Neville Spearman, 1969; London: Futura Publications, 1974.

Buttlar, Johannes v. *Schneller als das Licht*. Vienna: Econ Verlag, 1972.

Buttlar, Johannes v. *Journey to Infinity*. London: Fontana, 1976.

Buttlar, Johannes v. *Immortality*. New York: Bantam, 1976.

Buttlar, Johannes v. *Time-Slip*. London: Sidgwick & Jackson, 1979.

Condon, Edward U. *Scientific Study of Unidentified Flying Objects*. New York: Bantam, 1969; London: Vision Press, 1970.

Drake, W. Raymond. *Gods and Spacemen in the Ancient West*. London: Sphere, 1974.

Edwards, Frank. *Flying Saucers: Here and Now!* New York: Bantam, 1967.

Fry, Daniel. *The White Sands Incident*. Louisville, Ky: Best Books, 1966.

Fuller, John Grant. *The Interrupted Journey*. New York: Dial Press, 1966.

Hermann, Joachim. *Das falsche Weltbild: Astronomie und Aberglaube*. Munich: Deutsche Taschenbuch Verlag, 1973.

Hobana, Ion, and Weverbergh, Julien. *U.F.O.s from behind the Iron Curtain*. London: Souvenir Press, 1974; London: Corgi, 1975.

Holzer, Hans. *The Ufonauts*. Greenwich, Conn: Fawcett, 1976.

Hynek, J. Allen. *The U.F.O. Experience: A Scientific Inquiry*. Chicago:

THE U.F.O. PHENOMENON

Henry Regnery; London: Abelard–Schuman, 1972; London: Corgi, 1974.

Jacobs, David Michael. *The U.F.O. Controversy in America.* Bloomington, London: Indiana University Press, 1975.

Jung, Carl G. *Flying Saucers: A Modern Myth of Things Seen in the Skies.* Transl. R.F.C. Hull. London: Routledge & Keegan Paul, 1959.

Keel, John A. *U.F.O.s: Operation Trojan Horse.* London: Souvenir Press, 1971; London: Abacus, 1973.

Keyhoe, Donald E. *Flying Saucers from Outer Space.* London, New York: Wingate-Baker, 1969.

Keyhoe, Donald E. *Aliens from Space.* New York: New American Library, 1974; St Albans: Panther, 1975.

Klass, Philip J. *U.F.O.s: Identified.* New York: Random House, 1968.

Lorenzen, Coral, and Lorenzen, Jim. *U.F.O.s: The Whole Story.* New York: New American Library, 1969.

Menzel, Donald. *Flying Saucers.* Cambridge, Mass: Harvard University Press, 1953.

Menzel, Donald, and Boyd, Lyle G. *The World of Flying Saucers.* Garden City, N.Y.: Doubleday, 1963.

Puccetti, Roland. *Persons.* London: Macmillan, 1968.

Ruppelt, Edward J. *The Report on Unidentified Flying Objects.* Garden City, N.Y.: Doubleday; London: Gollancz, 1956.

Sagan Carl. *The Cosmic Connection.* Garden City, N.Y.: Doubleday; Sevenoaks: Coronet Books, 1973; New York: Dell, 1975.

Saunders, David R., and Hawkins, R. Roger. *U.F.O.s? Yes! Where the Condon Committee Went Wrong.* New York: New American Library, 1968.

Sigma, Rho. *Forschung in Fesseln.* Ventla Verlag, 1972.

Stanford, Ray. *Socorro Saucer in a Pentagon Pantry.* Austin, Texas: Blueapple Books, 1976. Revised edition: *Socorro Saucer.* London: Fontana, 1978.

Stringfield, Leonard H. *Situation Red: The U.F.O. Siege!* Garden City, N.Y.: Doubleday, 1977; London: Sphere, 1978.

Vallée, Jacques. *The Invisible College.* New York: Dutton, 1975. Published in Britain as *U.F.O.s: The Psychic Solution.* St Albans: Panther, 1977.

Vallée, Jacques. *Anatomy of a Phenomenon.* Chicago: Henry Regnery, 1965; London: Neville Spearman, 1966; London: Tandem, 1974.

A.P.R.O. Bulletin. 1954–78.

Flying Saucer Review. 1960–78.

U.F.O.-Nachrichten. 1978.

Index